Praise for *Vote Her In*

"As president of Cook County, the second-largest county in the United States, I know how important it is for women to be in executive decision-making governmental positions. Women in positions of leadership bring an important perspective too often lacking in our male colleagues. Rebecca Sive has made the case convincingly in *Vote Her In* for increasing the number of women in such governmental roles, which will surely lead to better lives for America's families everywhere."

　　—**Toni Preckwinkle**, president, Cook County Board of Commissioners

"*Vote Her In* bravely takes up women's political drama where the story left off in November 2016. It is the necessary call to action at the highest level to take the highest jobs in the land, including the presidency. Sive uses resources old and new—including the wonderful posters from the women's marches—to create a substantive and appealing guide for this last push. We can do it."

　　—**Linda Hirshman**, *New York Times* bestselling author, *Sisters in Law*

"An inspiring, savvy, and persuasive take on why America needs more female leadership now. Sive offers not just the analysis, but also the practical steps every woman and man can take to help women get into the C-suite and the Oval Office—and she argues that the time to do it is now."

　　—**Jessica Yellin**, former chief White House correspondent, CNN

"Far too few women, especially women of color, have the opportunity to become political leaders. This is a great loss to our nation that ought to be remedied as soon as possible. Let's #VoteHerIn, as Sive's inspirational guide so powerfully argues."

　　—**Kimberly M. Foxx**, state's attorney, Cook County, Illinois

"An indispensable tool for activists of all ages and experience levels."

　　—**Julie Scelfo**, journalist, activist, and author, *The Women Who Made New York*

"Blending eye-opening gender-bias statistics with inspiring sheroes from Abigail Adams to Mavis Staples to the Notorious RBG, Sive clearly shows the only path to equality requires electing Madam President."

　　—**Jessica Spring** and **Chandler O'Leary**, coauthors, *Dead Feminists*

"Sive takes her years of dedication to advancing women's political careers and causes and turns them into a call to action—along with some of the practical tools needed for real and rapid progress."

　　—**Katherine Baicker**, dean, University of Chicago Harris School of Public Policy

"Rebecca astutely explores a critical question: If we believe in justice for every American, will we work to elect women to public offices across the country, including the presidency? We must!"

—**Lisa Madigan**, attorney general, Illinois

"The United States is ready to elect our first woman president. We proved that in 2016. My friend Rebecca has now given us the new campaign plan. Let's do it!"

—**Congresswoman Jan Schakowsky**, US representative from Illinois

"An ironclad argument for why the United States needs to up the number of women in elected office."

—**Helaine Olen**, blogger, *Washington Post*, and author, *Pound Foolish*

"An incisive, powerful guide to democratic action."

—**Aviva Rosman**, COO, BallotReady

"A persuasive and inspirational visual and political manifesto reminding us that what we really need to fix this nation is one strong, competent woman in charge."

—**Robin Marty**, author, *Crow After Roe*

"Combining her years of political expertise and insightful interviews, Sive lays the groundwork for a plan that we can use to get more women in executive leadership roles in our government."

—**Anna M. Valencia**, city clerk of Chicago

"The rising of women can mean the rising of us all. Sive knows how to make that happen!"

—**Heather Booth**, award-winning civil rights activist, feminist, and political strategist

"Sive's passion for action leaps out of these pages. Her message is straightforward: Don't give up! Keep climbing up! Run to win! Run to lead! Inspire by example!"

—**Ruth B. Mandel**, professor and director, Eagleton Institute of Politics, Rutgers University

"A must-read for anyone who wants to understand why the United States has fared so poorly with regard to gender parity in political leadership."

—**Anne Moses**, president and founder, IGNITE

"Chock-full of helpful tips and actions, and inspired by the protest signs seen at the 2017 Women's March in Chicago, Sive gives us a colorful, hopeful viewpoint on why we need to vote a woman into the White House once and, especially, for all."

—**Erin Vilardi**, founder, VoteRunLead

VOTE HER IN

VOTE HER IN

YOUR GUIDE TO ELECTING OUR FIRST WOMAN PRESIDENT

REBECCA SIVE

MIDWAY

AN AGATE IMPRINT

CHICAGO

Printed in the United States of America

Images based on photography by Rebecca Sive of posters from the 2017 Chicago Women's March.

Madam President, from *She the People: Girlfriends' Guide to Sisters Doing It for Themselves*, printed with permission from The Second City, Chicago.

Image of Planned Parenthood button by permission of Planned Parenthood of Illinois.

Image on page 39 based on design by Hayley Gilmore and used with permission.

First Printing: October 2018

Library of Congress Cataloging-in-Publication Data

Names: Sive, Rebecca, author.
Title: Vote her in : your guide to electing our first woman president / Rebecca Sive.
Description: Chicago : Midway Books, [2018] | Includes bibliographical references.
Identifiers: LCCN 2018032144 (print) | LCCN 2018034701 (ebook) | ISBN 9781572848238 (e-book) | ISBN 1572848235 (e-book) | ISBN 9781572842618 (pbk.) | ISBN 157284261X (pbk.)
Subjects: LCSH: Women public officers--United States. | Women legislators--United States. | Women presidents--United States. | Women--Political activity--United States.
Classification: LCC HQ1391.U5 (ebook) | LCC HQ1391.U5 S58 2018 (print) | DDC 320.082/0973--dc23
LC record available at https://lccn.loc.gov/2018032144

10 9 8 7 6 5 4 3 2 1   18 19 20 21 22

Midway Books is an imprint of Agate Publishing. Agate books are available in bulk at discount prices. Learn more at agatepublishing.com.

For Steve Tomashefsky:
I am deeply grateful for your
constant and intelligent care.
Thank you.

"My fellow Americans. Vice President Warren. Speaker of the House Beyoncé.

The state of the union is . . . strong 'cause a woman is finally running shit.

Tonight marks the first time a woman delivers the State of the Union address. I follow forty-four white men and one black man. . . .

We have enacted universal health care and protected a woman's right to choose.

We have forgiven all student loans, made college education free, and we have raised salaries so that now each public school teacher makes at least twice as much as her shittiest ex-boyfriend.

Finally, we have passed legislation focused on equality—the Equal Pockets Law, which requires all women's pants, skirts, and dresses to have pockets.

How have we made all these gains possible? Through the creation of a simple tax I call the Actually Tax. Every time a man directs a sentence at a woman starting with the word *actually*, he pays one dollar.

So far, we have collected $8 trillion. Now, please join me in our updated pledge of allegiance, 'Run the World.'"

—Madam President, from *She the People:*
Girlfriends' Guide to Sisters Doing It for Themselves
THE SECOND CITY, CHICAGO

"In this country, everybody is supposed to be able to run for president, but that has never really been true."

—The Honorable Shirley Chisholm, *The Good Fight*, 1973
MEMBER, US HOUSE OF REPRESENTATIVES, 1968–1983
CANDIDATE FOR PRESIDENT OF THE UNITED STATES, 1972

"In light of this last election, I'm concerned about us as women and how we think about ourselves and about each other.... What is going on in our heads where we let that happen, you know?... When the most qualified person running was a woman and look what we did instead, I mean that says something about where we are.... That's what we have to explore ... if we still have this crazy, crazy bar for each other that we don't have for men ... if we're not comfortable with the notion that a woman could be our president compared to what, ... we have to have that conversation with ourselves as women."

—Michelle Obama, United State of Women Summit;
Los Angeles, California; May 5, 2018
FIRST LADY OF THE UNITED STATES, 2009–2017

CONTENTS

FOREWORD BY JULIA M. STASCH | xii

INTRODUCTION | I

PART ONE: We're Still Here | 8

CHAPTER 1:   We Hold These Truths to Be Self-Evident | 18

CHAPTER 2:   Could Be Asleep, Forced Me to Protest | 24

CHAPTER 3:   They Tried to Bury Us. They Didn't Know
               We Were Seeds | 30

CHAPTER 4:   This Pussy Grabs Back | 36

CHAPTER 5:   The Patriarchy Ain't Gonna Smash Itself | 45

CHAPTER 6:   We're Not Billionaire White Men | 50

CHAPTER 7:   Build Bridges, Not Walls | 56

CHAPTER 8:   Dear Trump: You Got 99 Problems and This
               BITCH Is 1 | 62

CHAPTER 9:   Hear Us Holler | 68

CHAPTER 10:   Beyoncé Runs the World | 74

CHAPTER 11:   Flag Day | 80

CHAPTER 12:   History Has Its Eyes on All of Us | 86

PART TWO: I Am Done Being Quiet | 92

CHAPTER 13: There Is No Wrong Way to Be a Woman
             (Unite) | 100

CHAPTER 14: The Future Is Nasty *(Name the Enemy)* | 108

CHAPTER 15: It Is Time to Use Our Outside Voices
             (Speak) | 118

CHAPTER 16: I Am Not Free While Any Woman Is Unfree
             (Connect) | 126

CHAPTER 17: Respect Existence or Expect Resistance
             (Resist) | 132

CHAPTER 18: Not Afraid *(Fight)* | 140

CHAPTER 19: I'm With Her *(Believe)* | 148

CHAPTER 20: Make America Think Again *(Educate)* | 154

CHAPTER 21: Words Matter *(Write)* | 162

CHAPTER 22: We'll See You in Court *(Litigate)* | 168

CHAPTER 23: We Are in This Together *(Elect Yourself)* | 176

CONCLUSION: Women Together Forward | 186

RESOURCES | 190

ENDNOTES | 205

BIBLIOGRAPHY | 223

ACKNOWLEDGMENTS | 239

FOREWORD

Yes, it's time—time for a woman to be president. It's *been* time at least since the Nineteenth Amendment was ratified granting American women the right to vote; it's *been* time at least since the campaign to pass the Equal Rights Amendment began. When *Vote Her In* author Rebecca Sive and I met during that first ERA ratification campaign, we couldn't see this day, but we knew it would arrive. And it has—time for a woman to be president.

It's time for all the reasons *Vote Her In* makes patently clear. The power and the strategy to elect a woman president are within reach. Women are ready, willing, and demonstrably able to exercise executive political power. It's time: yes, generated by anger, frustration, impatience, and ambition, but also by confidence and a deep concern that we are not using all the smarts, the savvy, the passion, and the leadership required to ensure that all people have a chance to succeed in our country and in an increasingly complex, changing, and confounding world.

It's time to move beyond the anger and protests (yes, satisfying, but . . .), beyond the infighting, the imposter syndrome, the fear of consequences, to a clear-eyed, methodical, no-holds-barred campaign to elect her. Let's do that because, as *Vote Her In* asserts, "electing a woman president will make all Americans better off." Let's elect her to prove to every woman and girl that she can aim high and succeed; that the journey from class president, to block club leader, to school board member, to city council, to state legislator, and beyond, pays off; and that the prize is worth the effort because executive political power matters in the lives of every American. Other countries have elected her; we can, too.

We need to get this elusive "first" behind us. The election and presidency of Barack Obama ripped off the Band-Aid of complacency about race in our country, forcing us to confront the malignant racism that threads through our history and continues today. Ugly, yes, but there is today perhaps a more honest environment within which to try to find common ground, to make progress, and to heal.

Although the #MeToo movement provides a jumpstart, the presidency of a woman may serve the same revolutionary purpose as the election of our first African American president. Let's face head-on the misogyny, the entitlement, the low expectations, and the patronizing "respect" for women that has made our path to shared power so hard.

There is one more important reason. A just society demands it. A just society is dedicated to the common good, to empathy, and to an acknowledgment of our shared humanity. My experience in government at the national and local levels, in the private and nonprofit sectors, and in philanthropy has made it clear that a just society requires that we tackle and remove the barriers to equal access, treatment, consideration, and opportunity.

The election of the first woman president is a building block of a just society. Let's build that society together.

Julia M. Stasch

PRESIDENT
JOHN D. AND CATHERINE T. MACARTHUR FOUNDATION

The views expressed herein are the personal views of Ms. Stasch and are not intended to reflect the views of the MacArthur Foundation.

INTRODUCTION

"GIRLS CAN BE ANYTHING, JUST NOT PRESIDENT"

—NEW YORK TIMES, NOVEMBER 10, 2016

We need to elect the first woman US president as soon as possible. This book presents the many reasons why her election will help every woman and the actions every woman can take to vote her in. No matter where you come from or how you define yourself, *Vote Her In* is your guide to winning our revolution— one as necessary as America's first.

This book contends that the very best strategy for creating a land of equal opportunity and justice *for all* is electing our first woman president, and that Madam President will improve every woman's life because the cornerstone of our democracy is its commitment to fairness and equality *for all*. Further, when a woman is POTUS, no one will be able to plausibly argue that women are unqualified to hold executive positions. Specifically, the election of Madam President will pave the way for more women attaining executive political and governmental power, which will demonstrate that gendered roles have no place in today's politics or governments.

"It all gets back to the land of equal opportunity," Illinois Attorney General Lisa Madigan told me in an interview. "It's not, and the men in power don't want to give it up. It has to be taken." This book explains why and how that taking should happen now.

"Yes, *she* can" is the message. Almost one hundred years since suffrage, American women are still making only incremental progress in winning political office, whether legislative or executive. Yet, as we'll see, research has shown that far more than their male colleagues, it is women public officials who advocate family-friendly policies that benefit women and girls. Women also bring different life knowledge, skills, and sympathies to political office, and they can apply that knowledge and those skills to changing the world for the better for all. And executives, beginning in the Oval Office, have a unique ability to promulgate such policies.

Many of us expected to elect our first woman president in 2016. In fact, as I'm sure you are aware, the majority of American voters wanted to vote her in then. But, instead of the favored candidate, Hillary Clinton, we got Donald Trump and his anti-woman behavior, legislative proposals, and executive actions.

Nevertheless, we persist: we are resisting by protesting, organizing, and advocating women's rights and opportunities. This rising-up started with the historic Women's March of 2017 ("the largest single-day [nationwide] protest in US history"), and it hasn't stopped.

"As the saying goes, 'You can't be what you can't see.' The idea, of course, is that until that highest ceiling is cracked, until there is a female president, we will never change the reality that for most Americans, leadership is synonymous with maleness."

—JESSICA BENNETT, *New York Times*, November 10, 2016

I have been thinking about the dearth of women in executive political office for many years. While I was teaching women's political leadership courses at the University of Chicago Harris School of Public Policy, I dug deep into the political science literature, media coverage of women in politics, and other writings on gender issues. The more I read, the more I found myself puzzling over the significance of the fact that in the United States, women don't hold executive political office in any significant numbers. Worse yet, too much of the time, they can't even get positioned to run for such offices.

In 2015, in anticipation of Clinton's run for the presidency, I created and taught a course at the University of Chicago titled Women in Executive and Governmental Political Leadership. I created it because I realized that the notion of women holding executive political office—so different from legislative office, which is where most women are elected—would be foremost once Clinton broke that highest glass ceiling and became a nominee for the presidency, as it seemed likely she would.

Eighteen months after teaching the course, two days after Clinton lost the 2016 presidential election, I read the following sentence in a *New York Times* op-ed: "The idea, of course, is that until that highest ceiling is cracked, until there is a female president, we will never change the reality that for most Americans, leadership is synonymous with maleness."

Executive power is the holy grail of politics and government. That's why electing an African American POTUS was such a big deal. As you think about that very big deal, remember this: the US Constitution stated that an African American was three-fifths of a person. The elemental obstacle to Barack Obama's election, or to the election of anyone else who looked like him, was not policy differences but his very being.

Likewise, evidently, for Clinton. Her very being was the problem. She is a woman, which is apparently even worse than being a *man of color*. Twice, she, a person with substantial public service, professional experience, and qualifications for the presidency, was defeated by a less-qualified man. Apparently, the American presidency, the ultimate expression of executive political power, is not considered fit for a woman. What other conclusion can one draw?

Time to not just teach a course but also to write a book.

Since moving to Chicago in 1973, I have worked as an organizer for women's equality and social justice. I have founded a women's center and have served as a public official, a philanthropic foundation director, and a volunteer leader of many organizations and projects, both in Chicago and nationally. I know how to create and mobilize political messages and movements that benefit women. And I wrote a book, *Every Day Is Election Day: A Woman's Guide to Winning Any Office, from the PTA to the White House*, which explains, step-by-step, how women who want to run for office can win. Now, with this book, those who don't want to run can join those who do to vote her in.

I began writing *Vote Her In* after attending the 2017 Chicago Women's March. It became clear to me there that marching could have a bigger payoff for American women than we had ever imagined before. No other political movement could have the same possibility of healing the rifts created by Trump's campaign and election and bringing every woman together in common cause. No other political context would present an equivalent opportunity for millennial, Gen X, and Gen Z women to join older women activists in the battle the baby boomers, their mothers, their grandmothers, and their great-grandmothers (whose activism was pre-suffrage) began but haven't finished: electing our first woman president.

However, I admit that when I first heard about the 2017 Women's March, I wasn't all that excited. I thought, what's another march when Trump's election has made me and everyone I know scared to get up each morning and read the day's headlines? I thought, how will Americans find the energy and spirit required to organize a march, let alone maintain that energy through all that will likely follow? But attending the 2017 Chicago Women's March and observing millions of other women across the United States (and around the world) with the same commitment to women's equality confirmed for me that women are determined and willing to elect Madam President. As the marchers said and I discuss later: it's time for pussy to grab back and start this revolution.

It's time to beat the boys for good and all and elect Madam President. Attorney General Madigan spoke for millions when she said to me, "I want it to happen in my lifetime." Then, for the first time since the nation's founding almost 250 years ago, a woman would lead our government and shape our country's and the world's future—likely for the better, if past policy making by American women in government is any indication. At long last, Americans would see what so many other nations around the world already know: women can be strong and effective executive, political leaders, too, and because they are so often committed to helping women and girls lead better lives, they uniquely change the world for the better.

Of course, let's continue to support other women's campaigns. Of course, let's run ourselves. But let's also do this: come together and win the presidency for every woman. I'm thinking of you,

- the millions who marched;
- the untold numbers who couldn't march but who share the marchers' sentiments;
- the millions who have been motivated by the #ShePersisted, #TimesUp, and #MeToo movements to advocate for women's rights;
- the millions of women who don't want their 2016 vote to be for naught;
- the hundreds of thousands of members and donors to women's advocacy organizations that fight to expand and preserve our rights;
- the hundreds of thousands of women—from high schoolers to the elderly—who lead community projects such as #NeverAgain, Indivisible chapters, and Black Lives Matter;
- the tens of thousands of women now training to run for public office; and
- the millions of millennial women about to replace my generation, the baby boomers, as the largest potential cohort of voters and political activists in the run-up to the next presidential election. You can do something we couldn't—by building on our successes, you can elect the first American woman president.

The graphic and narrative thread for *Vote Her In* was inspired by the imagery and messages of the handmade posters from the 2017 Chicago Women's March, which I photographed. The titles of Part One (the why) and Part Two (the how) are taken from those posters, as are the chapter titles. Last, a message from one of the March's posters is the title of the book's Resources section, a comprehensive list of media on women's history and politics, women's political art, and inspiring books for aspiring girl leaders.

Vote Her In also includes smart and inspirational advice from three of my good friends and colleagues who presently hold executive governmental office:

Kimberly (Kim) M. Foxx, state's attorney for Cook County, Illinois, which includes Chicago (according to Foxx, she is one of only a handful of women of color who currently hold office as elected prosecutors in the United States); City Clerk of Chicago Anna Valencia (according to Valencia, the first Latina to serve as legislative counsel and head of government affairs for a Chicago mayor); and Attorney General Madigan, now in her fourth term and one of the youngest American women to ever hold such a post.

I write the case for this herstory hoping that the first American woman president will be a woman who is committed to women's equality and policies that unquestionably benefit every woman. However, if the nation were to elect as its first woman president a woman who has not made this commitment explicitly, I believe the nation would still win; she would still demonstrate women's fitness for executive governmental office and, if history is any guide, she likely would advocate policies beneficial to women and work across party lines to do so.

Undoubtedly, as we march together along this campaign trail, we will differ on policy directions from time to time, sometimes significantly. But as I argue in the chapters that follow, I believe that, overall, Madam President will benefit all of us, and, therefore, all of us should participate in the campaign to elect her. Let's come together and undo the conventional wisdom that says a woman cannot be president. Yes, *she* can.

PART ONE

This book is a declaration of independence for our new American revolution, the one to elect the first American woman president now. Fervently, unapologetically, and clear-eyed, we begin with the case statement in Part One. This case statement, declaring we're still here and we're not going anywhere, explains why electing our first woman president is the best strategy for women to achieve full equality in the United States and argues that there is no time like the present to get it done.

If you are reading this manifesto, you are likely already committed to this movement, but here, you will find the argument for it, as well as the facts and the patriarchy-smashing proof points supporting not just another "Year of the Woman" but a new American revolution. Each chapter focuses on one aspect of the argument. You will find a lot of inspirational women's stories here, along with facts and figures that support the case for Madam President. Use these to convince your sisters and brothers to join you in this revolution.

I am confident that by the time you have marshaled this case and are ready to campaign to elect our first woman president, you will also appreciate the profound truths that buttress this call to action to vote her in. To start, American government executives are responsible for our well-being in ways that legislators just aren't. They:

- have administrative, management, and appointive powers that legis-lators do not;
- create and sign "executive orders," policy directives that have the force of law;
- have policy-making opportunities that legislators do not; and
- embody a polity and its purposes. Affirming the importance of this role, once we elect Madam President, women can "symbolize the nation," as State's Attorney Kim Foxx put it.

POTUS possesses these responsibilities in unique measure. This truth substantiates why my colleagues consistently stressed in my interviews with them the following points regarding the importance of electing our first woman president:

- **It would demonstrate that women can wield executive power as expertly as men can.**
- **It would prove that women can do anything.** Then, every woman would be able to tell any other woman or girl that she can be anything and not be lying. As Attorney General Lisa Madigan said,

"Until there is a woman president, you won't realize you really can do everything."

- **It would establish that women and their concerns and culture are important in every context.** "Women's voices will permeate the discussion in meaningful ways," according to State's Attorney Foxx.
- **It would clarify that every woman will be better off than she was before because women public officials consistently shape and advance policies beneficial to women.** As State's Attorney Foxx phrased it, most women work "to make sure [that] all boats are rising, that all policies work for everyone," and that every policy proposal is examined "through the eyes of being a woman."

I know that for those of us who are passionate about electing our first woman president, Hillary Clinton's loss still feels like a death in the family. We knew then—and still know now—that the rejection of her was a rejection of us and our beliefs. The 2017 Women's March reflected our frustration and sadness. But the mourning period has ended, and our sadness has turned to anger and action. American women have recognized that the mercurial man who was elected instead, who has no apparent respect for women or commitment to helping the people who elected him, must be stopped.

Happily, there is hope to be found in the 2016 presidential election numbers. Clinton won the popular vote. A majority of women voters chose Clinton because they found her highly qualified and also understood the benefits of such a regime change, the revolution that electing a woman president of the United States would engender. Clare Foran wrote in the *Atlantic* that Clinton "succeeded in winning women who might have voted for the Republican candidate in any other election"—*this election* being the first time there was a woman nominee from one of the two major parties; I rest my case.

These women helped Clinton win the popular vote. Ostensibly, this voting majority preferred Clinton to Trump because of her policy agenda, which included clear and measured proposals for improving the lives of women and

AMERICAN *women* WILL·NOT·BE SILENT

girls. These voters recognized the symbolic value of a woman sitting *at the president's desk* in the Oval Office—apart from any specific agenda item, her presence there unceasingly makes the point that women matter as much as men. These voters also understood that other women would get the same idea once they saw the first Madam President: *Let's elect another woman now that we see the good work she has done. Maybe I can be that candidate.*

Yet, Clinton, who was as qualified to be POTUS as any man who has ever run for or held the office, was defeated by a man who was unqualified and just not suited to it. Thunderstruck by the 2016 presidential election's outcome, tens of millions of us were left to ponder our case for the regime change that hadn't happened. After witnessing the election of a man with no governmental experience or aptitude who feels no obligation to follow the rules or, apparently, to adhere to common notions of presidential behavior, it's time for us to try again.

But what to make of the fact that a majority of white women voters didn't vote for Clinton? Does this fact undermine my argument that *every* woman will benefit from electing our first woman president or that every woman should work to elect her? The answer is no. Not all African Americans share the same political views or take the same political actions, yet all benefit from civil rights laws that prohibit race discrimination. Likewise, all women, regardless of their politics, will benefit from the actions of a woman president, who will, if precedent holds true for women in elected office, pay more attention to women's and girls' needs and address them more forcefully.

Additionally, in the process of campaigning to elect our first woman president—just like in our campaign to elect our first African American president—people who weren't believers before may become believers now. Polls now show Trump's support slipping among white women in states he won in 2016. "Trump has slipped into a much more precarious position with these women: Gallup put his 2017 approval with them at 45 percent in Pennsylvania, 42 percent in Michigan, and 39 percent or less in Minnesota, Iowa, Ohio, and Wisconsin," according to an article in the *Atlantic*. "Compared to his 2016 vote, his 2017 approval among blue-collar white women in the Rustbelt represented some of his largest declines anywhere—18 percentage points in Ohio and 19 in Wisconsin and Minnesota."

This reality has been reflected in American women's political mobilization since Trump's election. Starting with the 2017 Women's March, this mobilization grew throughout the year as women decided to run for office in historic numbers and to take matters into their own hands, including marching again in 2018. More and more women have come to learn that political change is uniquely powerful and beneficial in every woman's life. Now they know the best way to counter the forces of misogyny, as expressed in the person and actions of Trump, is through political action.

When I attended the 2017 Chicago Women's March, I experienced a movement that was 250,000 people strong, in which almost every person carried a sign expressing a fervent desire for a different world—a world where women have equal opportunities and are treated equally in every setting. Marchers wanted regime change. They still do.

All *you* need to do to be a part of this regime change is believe that women deserve the same rights and opportunities as men and support this declaration of independence, of women, by women, and for women, to secure life, liberty, and the pursuit of happiness for all. And while you're committing to elect our first woman president, consider this: If a woman can be the nation's chief executive, who can argue plausibly that other women aren't qualified to hold other governmental executive offices or, for that matter, any institution's executive office? (After all, none of those is as important as the presidency.) Let's get started on making the case.

THE FACTS

Lest you doubt the importance of electing the first woman POTUS, consider these damning facts, drawn from data gathered by the Center for American Women and Politics (CAWP) of the Eagleton Institute of Politics at Rutgers University:

- In 2018, none of the mayors of the ten largest cities were women (except interim Phoenix, Arizona, mayor, Thelda Williams). Only 21.8 percent of the mayors of cities with populations over 30,000, which is 1,365 cities, were women. Of the one hundred largest cities, only 20 percent of the mayors are women.
- In 2018, only six US governors were women; only thirty-nine women have ever served as governor (all but three since 1975).
- It wasn't until 1993 that the total share of women in statewide elected office exceeded 20 percent, reaching a high of 28.5 percent in 2000.
- In 2018, only 23.1 percent of statewide executive offices were held by women, including just seven of fifty state attorneys general. Yet, that office is often a stepping-stone to higher executive office—so much so that in 2017, Democrats launched the 1881 Initiative "to ensure that in five years, at least half of the party's attorneys general will be women," the *New York Times* reported. As the *Times* pointed out, "The office of attorney general has often served as a stepping-stone to election as senator or governor, thanks to the executive power it wields and attention it draws from both donors and the news media."
- No woman was elected to the US Senate until 1948 without first having been appointed to fill her husband's seat. (See chapter 18 for this great election story.)

- In early 2018, only 20 percent of the US Congress (House and Senate) were women. Most of these women were in the Democratic minority, meaning there were few women in the Republican majority to promote to committee chair positions. But women are often excluded when Democrats hold the majority as well. Consider this episode in the debate over the Affordable Care Act and the failure to include an amendment on women's health: "In short, every person who held power to decide what stayed in and what was cut from the most significant legislation in a generation [i.e., those who were committee chairs] was a man."
- Few women rise to executive leadership roles in state legislatures, such as house or senate majority or minority leader. For instance, in my home state of Illinois, there has been only one woman majority leader of the state House of Representatives in its entire history, and she was appointed in 1997.
- No woman served on the US Supreme Court until Justice Sandra Day O'Connor's confirmation in 1981. Between O'Connor's retirement in 2006 and Justice Sonia Sotomayor's confirmation in 2009, Justice Ruth Bader Ginsburg was the only woman serving on the court—we're talking just ten years ago!
- Executive offices are appointed, yet no American woman served in a presidential cabinet until 1933, and the second didn't follow for another twenty years.
- And, of course, no major political party nominated a woman candidate for president until 2016.

WE HOLD THESE TRUTHS TO BE SELF-EVIDENT

CHAPTER 1

WE HOLD THESE TRUTHS TO BE SELF-EVIDENT

The marcher bearing the WE HOLD THESE TRUTHS TO BE SELF-EVIDENT poster went to a lot of trouble to make her sign. She really did not want us to miss her point. A set of American flags crowned the sign's quotation from the Declaration of Independence, which calls to mind the famous phrase that follows: "that all men are created equal." She was positing that, in the sense of the Declaration, every American is created equally; that every American has "unalienable Rights"; that every American woman should be equal to every American man in every matter of government and policy. But, as everyone knows—including the Women's March attendee who created the sign that inspired this chapter—this isn't the case in the United States. If it were, women would have been able to vote since the nation was founded and would hold executive governmental office today as a matter of course.

Let's look at the nation's other founding document, the Constitution. Article 2 begins: "The executive Power shall be vested in a President of the United States of America." There you have it, girlfriends: power with a capital *P* goes to the president. Yet, in this country where we say all are created equal and all have unalienable rights, no woman has ever had this Power. As a country, we simply cannot claim the self-evident truths and equal rights of all Americans enumerated in our founding documents until we elect a woman POTUS.

Pulitzer Prize–winning author Annette Gordon-Reed put her finger on how the history of American women's constitutional rights relates to the dearth of American women with executive political power. In her review of *What Happened*, Hillary Clinton's account of the 2016 presidential election, Gordon-Reed wrote: "As things turned out, cultural understandings about the electoral process [for the presidency] in relation to gender were more powerful than understandings about it in relation to race." She pointed out that these understandings have been true ever since the Fifteenth Amendment "gave newly freed black men [but not women] the right to vote in 1870"— as confirmed by the willingness of American voters to elect a black man as president but not a woman.

I have already shared some depressing data about the lack of women in elected executive office in American government. Further, it is only since the Nineteenth Amendment was ratified, less than a century ago, granting federal suffrage in 1920 to American women, that progress has been made in electing and appointing women to executive office in any meaningful numbers. The fact is that we women remain in largely secondary roles, and our progress continues to be in slow motion.

So what are we missing out on? What don't women get to do because so few hold executive elected office? Well, whether mayor, governor, or president, the executive officeholder acts to propose budgets, define the government's policy agenda, and decide how the government will be run and who will run it. Further, she appoints others to executive office to carry out her plans; speaks for the government in contexts in which no one else does; signs executive orders that have the force of law; and represents the government, its authority, and its purposes.

When women don't serve as governmental executives, their knowledge and perspectives are missing from these political and policy decisions. Further, women tend to govern differently from men. For instance, research cited in the *New York Times* showed that congresswomen are often "more collaborative and bipartisan" than their male peers and are "significantly more

Close to one hundred years after suffrage, which American women spent more than a century fighting for, there is still no woman president.

likely than men to sponsor bills in areas like civil rights, health and education." Women "push for far more policies meant to support women, children, social welfare and—when they're in executive positions—national security." The *Times* cited one study showing that "female governors devoted much more attention to social welfare issues than male governors did, even after controlling for political and situational factors." These truths don't mean that women officeholders are better than their male peers in a behavioral sense, but it does mean they are more committed to making sure that governmental policies benefit everyone, including every woman.

Golda Meir, the only woman to serve as prime minister of Israel and the third woman *ever* to serve as prime minister of *any* country (and *all* in my lifetime), is a personal hero of mine. A popular women's movement poster of the 1970s captured the reason why: across the bottom of the poster, under a picture of Meir, was the caption BUT CAN SHE TYPE?

Once, in response to a series of rapes committed throughout Israel, it was suggested to Meir that she impose a curfew on women. She replied, "Men are committing the rapes. Let *them* be put under curfew." In other ways governing much like her male peers, Meir apparently differed from them when it came

Congresswomen secure about 9 percent more funding for their districts and sponsor and cosponsor more bills on family and children's issues than their male counterparts.

to addressing sexual assault. I contend this difference was because she was a woman. I contend that it was for the same reason that, in March 2018, every single woman US senator signed a letter to Senate Majority Leader Mitch Mc-Connell and Senate Minority Leader Chuck Schumer, pleading with them to take up the issue of sexual assault in congressional offices.

In an October 2016 article in the *Guardian* noting the rise of women mayors around the world, Megan Barry, then the mayor of Nashville and Davidson County, Tennessee, (who subsequently resigned after she had an affair with a member of her security detail and pleaded guilty to the misuse of government funds to carry out the affair), recalled a moment from a recent visit to a job site. "There was a big sign that said, 'men working,'" she said, "so I asked the men I was with what was wrong with the sign, and some of them noticed it was old or that it was chipped, but they didn't notice the wording. We've now gone to [a] national standard of 'workers present' for all our signs in Nashville." *Women officeholders don't have to be perfect to do good. They just have to care about what's right for women.*

It makes sense that women officeholders are in a better position to identify policy changes that benefit women and girls. For instance, male-dominated governments too often fail to identify, accommodate, or even consider women's needs. For instance, too often, mothers walk around in a world that simply was not built with them and their children in mind. In the *Guardian* article about women mayors around the world, Sarah Childs, a professor of politics and gender at Bristol University, was quoted saying: "If you've never tried to put a buggy on a bus, you don't really understand what many women's experience of public transport is." She added that "there's a burgeoning argument for childcare to be thought about as infrastructure—not just roads and rail." Such policies can benefit men who care for children, too, yet another good reason to elect more women to public office.

Like the policy about sexual assault that Israeli chief executive Golda Meir proposed, so too would our American woman president likely think differently about women's sexual and maternal health. Recent evidence of this proposition surfaced when Senator Tammy Duckworth of Illinois noted she wouldn't be able to vote when she was breast-feeding because children weren't allowed on the floor of the US Senate. Duckworth asked Senator Amy Klobuchar of Minnesota, the senior Democratic senator on the Senate Rules Committee, to support a rule changing the policy, which was passed in April 2018. Like Senator Duckworth, the future first Madam President will bring a perspective to the Oval Office that is different from any of her predecessors' in important ways.

The *New York Times* article I referred to about women governing differently also noted that "institutional bias" against bills sponsored by women means these bills "are often gridlocked in committee, so they never make it to a vote." This is all the more reason to elect more women legislators and executives, including Madam President. A greater number of women legislators will be less likely to be stymied by male peers. How many challenges to policies benefiting women would then be overcome? How many stereotypes about women's inferiority to men would then be discarded? How many more women, whether they call themselves feminists or not, would be eager to seek public office in order to promote policies benefiting women and girls? How many more women interested in government and politics would think about executive roles, understanding the opportunities they represent and the good they could do if they could hold them?

We hold these truths to be self-evident that a woman should sit in the Oval Office—behind the desk.

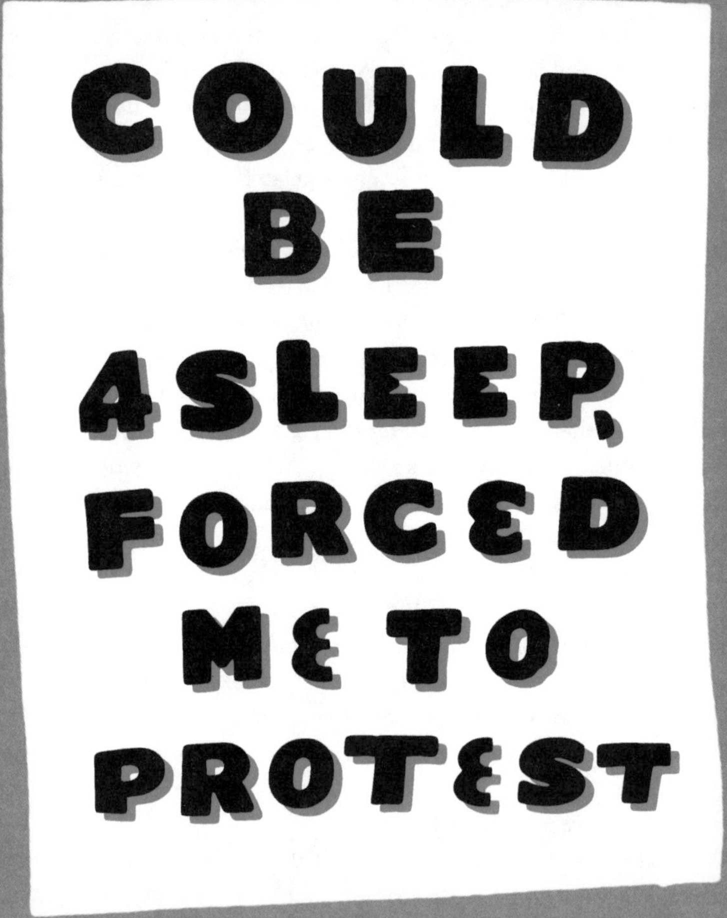
COULD BE ASLEEP, FORCED ME TO PROTEST

CHAPTER 2

COULD BE ASLEEP, FORCED ME TO PROTEST

At the beginning of my day at the 2017 Chicago Women's March, I saw a poster that read COULD BE ASLEEP: FORCED ME TO PROTEST leaning against a watercooler in a room set up for a Planned Parenthood breakfast. I stopped and thought, now isn't that right! We women sure do have some big, tiring problems on our hands. We might prefer to stay in bed, but we can't. We must act, beginning by taking heart from each other and the many courageous women of times past who also got up early to advocate women's rights.

What *does* make women get up and protest, as millions of us have done since Donald Trump was elected, as the poster maker so plaintively expressed? While the marcher I saw wished she could still be home in bed, nevertheless, she persisted—in glitter and color and all caps.

Thinking about what impels women to protest, I remembered the Second Wave feminists of the 1960s and '70s who called themselves witches, meaning women who woke up, spoke up, and protested injustice and inequality. This waking up to protest can take many forms, including our campaign to elect Madam President, but it begins with the courage to be a witch—to speak up and act out.

Almost three hundred years before the Second Wave feminists, the word *witch* held a different meaning for women in America. From what I remember from my elementary school history lessons on the Salem witch trials, the spin was that those who accused women of being witches—the men who put women on trial and then executed them—just didn't know any better, really. It was a long time ago, and those people weren't as civilized as we are today. It was all just a misunderstanding, this blaming of women who spoke out against society's problems—no big deal; our country has progressed to a better place since then (not so much).

It was only when I became a feminist myself in my early twenties (though I had exhibited a feminist's independence and fight for fairness much earlier in an argument over girls' participation in my elementary school's kickball team) that I heard the term *witch* again. Feminist friends were forming covens, which were women's clubs, just by another name. The covens involved women getting together to work to make their communities better. These women realized that naming themselves "witches" was clear code for women who speak up, stand out, and denounce anti-women behavior—just like those women in Salem. Witches they would be.

An article about WITCH, one such feminist group formed in New York and Chicago in the late 1960s, described the organization this way: "The group specialized in disruption of the sensational bent, shrieking and chanting in black clothing and white face paint, and 'throwing hexes' at enemies of the people. Among their many targets were beauty pageants, Wall Street, bridal fairs, Chase Bank, the presidential inauguration, and even sexists in the politically left anti-war movement. Some of the more famous work was actually quite modest in its goals (hey, all politics are local politics)."

Here is part of a "hex" a group from the Chicago WITCH branch apparently sang at a protest about the cost of riding public transportation run by the Chicago Transit Authority (CTA):

Witches round the circle go
to hex the causes of our woe,
We the witches now conspire
To burn CTA in freedoms' fire.

NO WOMAN CAN CALL HERSELF FREE WHO DOESN'T OWN AND CONTROL HER BODY!

The article also noted that WITCH is one of many feminist groups that is "sadly understudied and overlooked," adding that "it's baffling to think that explicitly socialist groups like WITCH and the Chicago Women's Liberation Union started out on the same footing as Hillary Clinton boosters like the National Organization for Women, but we all know that even in the feminist movement, the game is rigged towards Wellesley girls." Like Hillary Clinton. Which is a good thing.

I didn't connect all the dots in my own history with twentieth-century feminist witches until I read the paragraph above—the Chicago Women's Liberation Union was the first feminist group I joined. Most of my earliest Chicago women friends were also members. I remember task forces on issues like day care and jobs. And I remember the requirement that everything be decided by consensus. (Talk about subduing outspoken women—how ironic, as I reflect on that!) But I didn't remember the witches.

In an amusing synopsis of her 2013 book *Six Women of Salem: The Untold Story of the Accused and Their Accusers in the Salem Witch Trials*, author Marilynne K. Roach summed up in the *HuffPost* her sense of the history of the character and treatment of witches. For our purposes, this is the most salient characteristic she said could get a woman accused of witchcraft: "You are contentious and stubborn with a turbulent reputation." Could be asleep, forced me to protest, indeed.

Stacy Schiff's brilliant examination of the Salem witch trials, *The Witches: Suspicion, Betrayal, and Hysteria in 1692 Salem*, tells the horrifying yet entrancing stories of the so-called witches in deep and compelling detail. According to one critic, their stories can be summarized as "the worst misogynist atrocity in American history"—in which things went horribly wrong and, guess what, the men in power blamed the women without power. Nothing new or old there. Could be asleep, forced me to protest.

In a repeat of the 1960s and '70s, today's young women are also hopping on the witch train. In a November 2017 *New York Times* column titled "Season of the Witch," Michelle Goldberg wrote, "This assumption of chaos—the

> If calling yourself a witch makes you feel more powerful, call yourself a witch. Stand up; speak up; be argumentative; say that it's time for women to take charge, beginning in the Oval Office.

sense that institutions have failed and no one is in charge—helps explain the well-documented resurgence of occultism among millennials." I think this sense of institutions failing also explains why we're getting up early to protest. And, clearly, for millions of women, the ultimate institutional failure was the election of Donald Trump.

If calling yourself a witch makes you feel more powerful, call yourself a witch. Stand up; speak up; be argumentative; say that it's time for women to take charge, beginning in the Oval Office. Get up and protest for this cause, as long as is needed.

In her column, Goldberg cited a former witchcraft teacher who told her that witchcraft lets you be the "arbiter of your own justice." That justice is certainly what's needed now—best and fastest and most completely realized in executive governmental power, beginning with electing Madam President, who by her mere presence will change everything. Witches' curses are permitted, if they get us there faster.

CHAPTER 3

THEY TRIED TO BURY US. THEY DIDN'T KNOW WE WERE SEEDS

I am a passionate gardener, so I wait eagerly each spring to see what has survived from one year to the next. I am not always happy with the outcome. But I can say that the sense of renewal I get is always of equal measure. Life exists under all that midwestern snow and hard ground.

Each year, I go through the cycle of clearing, weeding, planting, mulching, and tending, which leads to blooming. Every spring, and then every summer, I experience the same sensation: I marvel to see the buried seeds break frozen ground and blossom. I gasp with joy at what persistence has created. Buried seeds will grow and blossom.

On its face, the term *burial* seems like an absolute: a person is buried, or not. But that's not right. While a body may be buried, memories of an individual never are. And in those memories is the living spirit of the deceased. Of course, the artifacts of that loved one may be around, too, always there to treasure, much like memories. When she lost the presidential election in 2016, Hillary Clinton didn't die, though her loss felt that way to millions. And, I think, that's why THEY TRIED TO BURY US: THEY DIDN'T KNOW WE WERE SEEDS was seen on posters at the 2017 Women's March protests all over the world. We know we need a woman president in order to fully bloom.

An enemy may try to bury us with vitriol, lies, and hateful actions; certainly, Donald Trump tried to do that to Hillary Clinton and her voters. But he failed. He didn't know that just as burying seeds won't stop them from growing, attacking women won't stop them from fighting for their dream. And because we grow again, we will clear away the debris. We will nurture. We will carry that dream in our hearts and minds and souls. Now is a new season. We will grow again.

The evocative phrase, "They tried to bury us: they didn't know we were seeds," seen on so many Women's March protest signs, is attributed to twentieth-century Greek poet Dinos Christianopoulos, an ostracized gay man who wouldn't be buried. When no one would publish his homoerotic poetry, he created his own publishing firm. Similarly, when Hillary Clinton lost her presidential run, American women created their own political force. We are self-starters, too, growing another campaign to elect Madam President.

This chapter recounts the story of one of our elder sisters, a woman who wouldn't be buried—so much so that she ran for president herself. She was Shirley Chisholm. She was "unbought and unbossed," claiming the presidency as American women's due as no woman had before her. In our campaign to elect Madam President, we would do well to follow her example.

Chisholm was born in 1924 to Caribbean immigrants in Brooklyn, New York, just four years after passage of the Nineteenth Amendment. After becoming the first African American congresswoman in 1968, she ran for the 1972 Democratic Party nomination for the presidency at age forty-eight. By that time, she had more experience in the federal government than, say, Barack Obama. Chisholm said it first: "Black male politicians are no different from white male politicians," she remarked during her presidential nomination campaign. "This 'woman thing' is so deep."

Chisholm began her career as a teacher and later served as director of a childcare center and an educational consultant while becoming a leader of a local Democratic Party club in Brooklyn and serving in the New York State

DEFLOWER the PATRIARCHY

Assembly. By the time Chisholm ran for the presidential nomination of a major American political party, the first African American to do so, she had served in the Assembly for three years, where she advocated for the rights of women domestic workers. She continued her advocacy for working women's rights when she served in the US House of Representatives for seven terms. While there, she cofounded the Congressional Black Caucus.

Chisholm is justly heralded for the courage she demonstrated in her presidential run, but she previewed that courage in her first congressional run, when her campaign slogan was that compelling phrase, "unbought and unbossed."

I think that any woman who has ever sought executive political or governmental leadership—as, I'm speculating, Chisholm already had in mind when campaigning for a congressional seat—believes she doesn't need to be "bossed"—that is, told what to do. In the context of New York City Democratic Party politics back in the day, Chisholm probably meant to convey to voters and political leaders who opposed her that the local Democratic political machine wasn't going to boss her around.

Chisholm embodied the notion, "They tried to bury us: they didn't know we were seeds" in important ways. For instance, throughout her political career—whenever she had to get something done she thought was important—she willingly and without fear challenged institutional (usually male) power to achieve her goals. If they tried to bury her, she would dig herself out.

For example, in her first congressional campaign, Chisholm ran in the Democratic primary as the outsider against three other black candidates, including a male judge and a male state senator. Her opposition thought they would bury her. Instead, she won the primary.

Then she prevailed in the general election over James Farmer, Jr., a well-known civil rights leader. When she wasn't appointed to the congressional committee she fought back again. (To better represent her constituents, Chisholm preferred to be on the Veterans' Affairs Committee, not the Agricultural Committee; as she put it: "There are a lot more veterans in my district than trees.") This time, she fearlessly sought counsel from two powerful men:

Robert Dole, then representing a Kansas congressional district, and Brooklyn Orthodox Jewish leader Rabbi Menachem M. Schneerson—but she sought their advice as leaders to be respected, not as bosses to be obeyed. Both encouraged her to think creatively about what she could do as a member of the Agriculture Committee to help her constituents and other Americans in need. This thinking resulted in the creation of the federal WIC program, which provides food to low-income mothers and children.

Bear in mind that at this time, there were eleven congresswomen, and Chisholm was one of only two women of color among them. (The other was Patsy Mink, a Japanese American who subsequently became a US senator from Hawaii.) Chisholm eventually was appointed to the Veterans' Affairs Committee.

One of the best parts of unbought and unbossed Chisholm's political career is that throughout her time in the House of Representatives, she hired only women staffers and, according to one source, half were African American. This was another way in which she refused to allow herself to be buried or ignored. Chisholm famously said once that she experienced more discrimination based on her gender than on the color of her skin: "When I ran for the Congress, when I ran for president, I met more discrimination as a woman than for being black. Men are men."

Men are men. Let that sink in.

"Men are men," of course, presaged the gendered presidential vote that came almost a half century later, in 2016. But what we also know from Shirley Chisholm's story is that the wise women who will elect our first woman president, along with the woman who will *be* our first woman president, will need to do like Chisholm did: convince the powerful to support the fight for justice while remaining unbought and unbossed in their messaging and deed. We must do like Chisholm did when her opposition thought it had buried her: grow again.

CHAPTER 4
THIS PUSSY GRABS BACK

I n October 2016, just a month before the presidential election, a 2005 video resurfaced of then presidential candidate Donald Trump describing how he views women. "And when you're a star, they let you do it. You can do anything," Trump told Billy Bush, then host of *Access Hollywood*. "Grab 'em by the pussy. You can do anything."

Grab 'em by the pussy.

This crass phrase heard around the world was brushed off by Trump (and many others) as "locker room banter." But for many of us, the behavior Trump described and the cruel and dismissive way he characterized it were emblematic of our worst fears about the man who could become our president—that he felt entitled to abuse women's bodies, that he believed women exist solely to serve men sexually. And when this man who spoke these words was elected to the highest office in the land, it was clear that systemic oppression of women wasn't going to be changed by *this man* in charge.

In response, during the weeks following Trump's election, women all over the country acted to reclaim "pussy." They made and wore "pussy hats" symbolizing their reclaiming. They made signs that countered Trump: THIS PUSSY GRABS BACK. The ultimate grab? Well, of course, that would be the presidency.

Donald Trump is not the first man with power to assert "grab 'em by the pussy" behavior. Our world is full of such men, as the #MeToo movement, the collective voice and pussy-grabs-back action of millions of women, has demonstrated.

Women have been grabbing back for centuries now. Jane Addams and Ida B. Wells—heroines of American women's march to equality in the late nineteenth and early twentieth centuries—would probably be appalled to learn that I'm writing about them in a chapter titled "This Pussy Grabs Back," but that's what they did—metaphorically speaking, anyway—showing the rest of us how to demand what *we're* entitled to. So that's why I am telling their stories here, as inspiration for maintaining a lifelong pussy-grabs-back mentality and for making the ultimate grab—for the presidency.

Jane Addams and her then personal companion, Ellen Gates Starr—then two young, middle-class, educated women who wanted to spend their lives bettering the world—founded Hull-House in Chicago in 1889. Hull-House was a US outpost of a worldwide social justice community, the settlement house movement, begun in London, England. It was located in a poor immigrant neighborhood on Chicago's Near West Side.

As Hull-House grew, it expanded its mission, becoming a catalyst for political action and policy changes to improve the lives of area residents and the living conditions in poor and immigrant Chicago neighborhoods. Addams and the other Hull-House staff, primarily women who lived at Hull-House, became leaders of various women's movements and social justice causes. These efforts culminated in Addams winning the Nobel Peace Prize in 1931 and President Franklin D. Roosevelt appointing Hull-House activist Frances Perkins as secretary of labor in 1933, the first woman to be a member of a presidential cabinet.

Like so many other American women who dared, who worked so hard and courageously, who led fight after fight so the rest of us could have better lives and more opportunities, Jane Addams's work and beliefs were sanitized. According to noted historian Anne Firor Scott, Addams's neighbors started calling her "Saint Jane," and the nickname stuck. How much safer and less

WOMAN'S PLACE IS IN THE RESISTANCE

Like so many other American women who dared, who worked so hard and courageously, who led fight after fight so the rest of us could have better lives and more opportunities, Jane Addams's work and beliefs were sanitized.

threatening it must have felt to describe Addams and the other young women who founded settlement houses, hotbeds of social justice and political organizing, as saints rather than to *accurately* describe them as community organizers fighting for political and economic justice!

Scott's 1960 article for *American Heritage* magazine, "Saint Jane and the Ward Boss," recounted the work of a pussy who fought back. In it, Scott described the process by which Addams, Starr, and other Hull-House residents came to understand the need for systemic political change: "They began to find out about the little children sewing all day long in the 'sweated' garment trade, and about others who worked long hours in a candy factory. They began to ask why there were three thousand more children in the ward than there were seats in its schoolrooms, and why the death rate was higher there than in almost any other part of Chicago. . . . (Once they traced a typhoid epidemic to its source and found the sewer line merging with the water line.)"

Scott recounted Addams's leadership, noting that by 1898, "after nine years of working with their [largely immigrant] neighbors [to improve their community], the Hull-House residents [led by Addams] were ready to pit their influence" against their corrupt—in their view—alderman and to "put up a candidate of their own." While the alderman prevailed and suggested that "bygones be bygones," according to Scott, "Addams was furious," and she wrote a letter that appeared in several of Chicago's newspapers "reaffirming the attitude of Hull-House toward [the alderman:] 'It is needless to state that the protest of Hull-House against a man who continually disregards the most fundamental rights of his constituents must be permanent.'"

Let me remind you that the "Hull-House" Addams named as an opposing body to the alderman was a group of mostly women who moved from individual acts of assistance in their work at Hull-House to group action in order to counter injustice. Let me further remind you that, at the time these women were organizing and leading opposition to a political candidate, they couldn't vote. Women's suffrage didn't become law until 1913 in Illinois for presidential elections only and in 1920 as a federal constitutional right. It was only in 1869, nine years after Addams was born and twenty years before Hull-House was founded, that married women—and only married women—in Illinois *were even granted property rights.*

Pussy sure did grab back when Addams and her community fought city hall.

Ida B. Wells was born a slave in 1862, and, like Jane Addams, she was raised in a family that valued education and civic engagement. (Addams's father served in the Illinois state legislature for many years.) During Reconstruction, Wells's father was a Republican Party activist committed to higher education. He was involved in the Freedmen's Aid Society and helped found Shaw University in Mississippi (now Rust College), which Wells attended. Wells's own activist spirit made an appearance in an important way when she was in her early twenties. While riding a train from Memphis to Nashville in 1884, Wells refused to move to the back of the train as the conductor demanded. She sued the railroad, ultimately losing the case, but her fortitude and willingness to grab back never left her.

Living in Memphis in 1892 and part owner of her own newspaper, the *Memphis Free Speech*, Wells was outraged and deeply distressed by the lynching of three local African American businessmen, whom she described as "three of our best young men." There, she began the anti-lynching movement that defined her life, moving, like Addams, from individual action to collective action to combat injustice until her death in 1931. She wrote, spoke, and organized advocacy campaigns, legislative efforts, and community betterment projects. She even ran for office. Whatever she could do, she would do.

During her anti-lynching campaign, Wells wrote an editorial in the *Memphis Free Speech* that caused an uproar among the city's white residents (according to my research, a copy of the editorial no longer exists). A mob rallied outside of the newspaper's office and threatened Wells that if she ever came back to Memphis, she would be killed. (She had been traveling to New York City at the time of the riot and did not return to Memphis.)

In February 1893, eleven months after the lynching, Wells gave a speech titled "Lynch Law in All Its Phases," in which she described the Memphis African American community's reaction to the lynching and its meaning:

> I have no power to describe the feeling of horror that possessed every member of the race in Memphis when the truth dawned upon us that the protection of the law which we had so long enjoyed was no longer ours; all this had been destroyed in a night, and the barriers of the law had been thrown down, and the guardians of the public peace and confidence scoffed away into the shadows, and all authority given into the hands of the mob, and innocent men cut down as if they were brutes.

These are the words of a pussy who grabs back.

After Wells became a leader of the anti-lynching movement, anti-lynching advocacy became a primary focus of "black women's clubs." By 1896, she had formed one such organization, the National Association of Colored Women.

Wells ultimately moved to Chicago, married, raised four children, and cofounded the NAACP. Addams was an early member of its board of directors.

Both Addams and Wells were interested in elected office, though as I mentioned, only Wells actually ran. Addams was appointed to governmental office, serving on the Chicago Board of Education and, in the early Hull-House years, as the garbage inspector for her ward.

What are we to make of Addams and Wells? For my part, I am awed by the lifelong commitment and nonstop energy and passion of these two women to support causes that benefit all. I am also in awe of their intellectual and political prowess, their compelling writing and speaking, and their mobilization of movements for justice. Always, they declared: here is what's wrong, here is why it's wrong, here is what we have to do about it, here I am to do my part.

That's how pussy (every woman) grabs back and makes the world better for all women.

First, we women need to stake out a position, as Wells and Addams did in their writing and speaking. Then, we mobilize, creating and leading organizations and movements to push for that named change—for instance, electing our first woman president.

In her first autobiography, *Twenty Years at Hull-House*, Addams described how the need to organize a movement, the settlement house movement—to grab back—became clear. She wrote that since nowhere "in Church or State are a body of authoritative people [men] who will put things to rights as soon as they really know what is wrong," she and her colleagues would found Hull-House.

Men weren't putting things right, so women did—just as we are today.

As Wells and Addams moved ever more deeply and unabashedly into catalyzing systemic change and becoming the voices of that change, they exemplified the message of this book: women en masse *can* change the system. As Wells wrote in her autobiography, *Crusade for Justice*, "One had better die fighting against injustice than to die like a dog or a rat in a trap" and "I'd rather go down in history as one lone Negro who dared to tell the

As Wells and Addams moved ever more deeply and unabashedly into catalyzing systemic change and becoming the voices of that change, they exemplified the message of this book: women en masse *can* change the system.

government that it had done a dastardly thing than to save my skin by taking back what I have said."

Today, our government is again doing a dastardly thing: systemically denying women equal opportunity and treatment. We can rectify this by grabbing back and electing our first woman president.

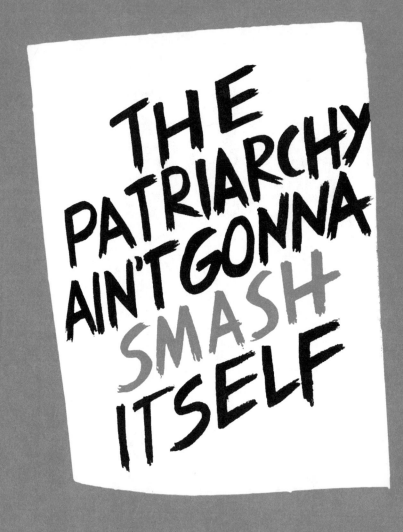

CHAPTER 5

THE PATRIARCHY AIN'T GONNA SMASH ITSELF

A t the end of 2017, author and journalist Susan Faludi wrote in an op-ed piece for the *New York Times* that "the patriarchy isn't going anywhere" as long as the primary form of women's activism "is an expression of direct anger at the ways individual men use and abuse us [rather than] fighting the ways the world is structurally engineered against women."

What Faludi called a world "structurally engineered against women" is the institutionalized decision-making structure—in every sector of our lives— that is controlled and run primarily by men. It is the patriarchy that needs to be smashed—as one Women's March sign put it—if women are to have equal rights and opportunities, including the opportunity to exercise the executive governmental power that shapes and rules our lives. Consequently, Faludi advocated, as I do here, that we get up, show up, and create systemic change.

But one point Faludi doesn't make in her op-ed that I do here is this one: the strategy to "smash" the patriarchy is available and actionable; this book presents it. It is electing the first American woman president, thereby demonstrating that the political patriarchy is not immutable. In her book *Women & Power: A Manifesto*, Mary Beard stated that after the patriarchy is smashed, there will be no more "female exteriority," her term to describe the idea that, as society is structured now, men are inside the power structures and women

are outside; therefore, women are always having to break down those struc-
tural barriers and the institutions that run their lives.

Marchers knew all about female exteriority. That's why so many of their posters proclaimed DEFLOWER THE PATRIARCHY and SMASH THE PATRIARCHY. Time to elect Madam President. The fact is that executive power in the American political system has been held almost exclusively by men since the nation's founding. *No matter what institutional sector of American society you study, you will find the same circumstance: there are few women with executive power and even fewer who are top executives. That's* the patriarchy to smash. I contend that smashing the presidential patriarchy will encourage women in other professions to take heart and fight the system that prevents them and their sisters from moving into executive positions.

> There are only 24 women CEOs in the Fortune 500.

Despite studies, speeches, conferences, workshops, and diversity and inclusion statements galore, the fact remains that sexism is embedded in American institutions, which are seemingly resistant to change by any means attempted so far.

As I shared earlier, CAWP has collected a lot of data that prove this point in the political context. In another comprehensive review, this one by the Pew Research Center, researchers found that no matter where they looked, the results were the same: men and women were subject to unequal expectations when it came to achieving positions of leadership, resulting in fewer women achieving executive leadership roles.

Here are some key facts on women's leadership from the Center for American Progress (CAP):

- American women hold almost 52 percent of all professional-level jobs but make up only 25 percent of executive- and senior-level officials and managers, 20 percent of board seats, and 6 percent of CEOs. (A *New York Times* story about the Glass Ceiling Index offered a comedic presentation of the magnitude of this problem: "Fewer Women Run Big Companies Than Men Named John.")

- Although women in the legal field make up 45 percent of associates, they account for only 22 percent of partners and 18 percent of equity partners.
- 37 percent of all physicians and surgeons are women, but only 16 percent of permanent medical school deans are women.

CAP concluded that for three decades, "women have outnumbered men on college campuses . . . yet they have not moved up to positions of prominence and power in America at anywhere near the rate that should have followed." CAP estimated that "at the current rate of change, it will take until 2085 for women to reach parity with men in key leadership roles in the United States." That won't be true for the presidency, if we have anything to do with it!

Imagine Inauguration Day: a woman stands up, speaks out, and symbolizes American nationhood. She might be wearing a pantsuit, she might be wearing a skirt or a dress, but her very *presence* will be what matters. For every woman, this moment will reinforce her personal sense of autonomy and the ability to rise. For every woman, this moment will clarify that it is communal action that creates revolutionary change: the patriarchy ain't gonna smash itself, but it can be smashed by our actions. For men and boys, this moment will underscore the fact that all humans have the capacity to govern. Their view matters, too.

Around the same time that Susan Faludi's article was published in the *New York Times*, Karen Tumulty, a *Washington Post* columnist covering national politics, wrote about the record number of women running for governor. She cited data collected by CAWP showing that, in January 2018, at least 79 women (composed of 49 Democrats and 30 Republicans) were running for governor in 2018 or seriously considering doing so ahead of filing deadlines. "Their candidacies are testing long-held attitudes about women and leadership," Tumulty wrote. She also quoted CAWP Director Debbie Walsh as saying that a run for governor "runs up against the stereotype to see women as the chief decider, the place where the buck stops." Then, Stacey Abrams, an African American woman, won the Democratic nomination for governor in Georgia, Michelle Lujan Grisham, a Latina, won the Democratic nomination for governor in New Mexico, and, according to the *New York Times*, "from Tuesday [June 12, 2018] through September [2018], female candidates for governor will be on the ballot in Democratic primaries across 17 states, including pivotal battlegrounds such as Florida, Wisconsin and Colorado—part of the record number of women running for governor this year." The ripple effect of these gubernatorial runs could reach the White House, as data support the notion that governors become presidents:

- Almost 38 percent of US presidents (17 of 45) previously served as the governor of a state.
- Four of the last seven presidents (Jimmy Carter, Ronald Reagan, Bill Clinton, and George W. Bush) were governors.

Yet, electing more women governors is likely to continue to be an incremental process. And while more women governors likely will mean more women seeking the presidency, that will probably be an incremental process, too. However, the fact that more women than ever before have expressed interest in running for governor—and are now running—suggests that women feel like they have "more political agency than in the past." There's no better time than now to elect more women governors to increase our chances of electing Madam President, demonstrating in the process that women can (and should) run any level of government.

US Representative Diane Black, the first woman to chair the House Budget Committee and a 2018 Republican candidate for governor of Tennessee, said this about her suitability for being governor: "Maybe it's because I was a single mom working the night shift as a nurse. It's just how I'm wired." Black was making the point that being a woman is an asset in policy making because she understands women's and families' needs.

I abhor Diane Black's antichoice, anti–Planned Parenthood platform, but if her experiences as a woman (i.e., as a single working mother) mean she's committed to using executive political power to benefit women economically, then I am with that part of her program. But, if at the same time she maintains her anti-Planned Parenthood stance, I would argue against it and fight to defeat such policy proposals. In this context, remember that electing (even) imperfect women governors who acknowledge that being a woman gives them a favorable policy perspective on some needs of women will at least begin the smashing of the patriarchy.

There's no time like the present to get started, for the patriarchy ain't gonna smash itself.

CHAPTER 6

WE'RE NOT BILLIONAIRE WHITE MEN

Because it is women public officials who typically propose and advocate policies that benefit women and no male president has made women's economic equality a reality, it's time to elect a woman president who would do everything in her power to put women on an equal economic footing with men. Ask any woman and she likely will be able to recount instances of workplace discrimination. That would include our future Madam President, making it all the more likely that she will make women's economic equality a priority.

In their posters, marchers clearly articulated the systemic discrimination women experience in the workplace, regardless of job, profession, race, ethnicity, or age. These inequities include profound wage disparities—78 CENTS TO HIS DOLLAR, as one Women's March poster proclaimed. The daily reality for many working women is gender-based job segregation and its concomitant lower pay, as well as other workplace inequities rooted in sex discrimination, and exacerbated by race discrimination, including sexual harassment.

The numbers tell this grim tale. Women make up approximately 47 percent of our country's workforce, yet they are often paid less than men and have fewer opportunities for advancement. More than 39 percent of women work in occupations where women represent at least three-fourths of the workforce. This occupational segregation results in lower wages in jobs where women predominate. Women are also more likely than men to work in low-wage jobs—they represent 19 million of the 23.5 million people working in low-wage, largely female-dominated occupations, according to a report by the Institute for Women's Policy Research. These women have little economic security or opportunity to move up the economic ladder, yet "demand for low-wage workers is expected to increase as time goes on, meaning more and more women—a disproportionate number of whom are immigrants and women of color—will be called to fill those roles." These are jobs where the median hourly wage for all workers is less than $15, and in which "just-in-time" scheduling, where workers learn their schedules as little as two hours before their shift, is common.

Compound the low-paid, segregated workplace reality for so many American women with the fact that American women who work outside the home—which includes 70 percent of mothers with children under 18—continue to do the majority of the work *inside* the home, too. This unequal burden exists both when a male partner is present in the home and when he is not (23 percent of American families are living in households headed by a single mother).

In this era when millions of American women are responsible for the majority of homemaking and childcare responsibilities, most earn little money, have minimal job mobility, and experience continuing gender-based workplace discrimination, including unequal pay for equal work. Because women have to work longer to make the same amount of money as men do, their capacity to engage in political and civic activities or contribute financially to such activities can be circumscribed. An unfortunate result is that women workers may not have as much time or money as their male coworkers to gain influential leadership or donor roles in political campaigns. And, of course, if you have spent *any* time on a political campaign, you know just how significantly money and time beget leadership and influence.

The wealthy white men who own and run most of America's biggest businesses have not shown significant interest in adopting pay or advancement policies that would engender equal economic opportunity or equal pay.

FiX WAGE DiSPARiTY

Instead, and seemingly with increasing frequency, these men are enriching themselves at the expense of their low-paid workers and, when they get tired of that or can't figure out how to spend all the money they earn, they are running for office, often without any prior political or government experience.

Typically, men like these choose offices where there is a potential for executive decision making, for example, mayor, governor, US Senate, and, oh yes, the presidency. After all, these men are used to being executives and making decisions of great import with minimal interference. Often, they self-fund their campaigns, enabling them to push others, including well-qualified women, out of races. (The average candidate for Congress may spend close to half her [or his] time raising money.)

Because only 25 percent of women are in the upper ranks of big companies, they have much less of a chance of becoming self-funding political candidates than men do, thereby making the pool of such women who might consider running for office much smaller.

Lest you think I am unduly criticizing white men, consider this: of the world's 2,043 billionaires in 2018, only eleven were black and 256 were women. My point is a straightforward one: white men control the economic reality that most women face, thereby limiting the pool of women who might share their wealth with women candidates or fund themselves in a political campaign. However, if forced to address Madam President, men might have to exert their economic power more equitably.

Despite these facts, the tens of thousands of American women who have said they want to run for office demonstrate just how motivated women are to effect social and political changes that benefit them, including electing our first woman president. They understand just how much government can help them lead more economically secure lives, starting with actions taken in the Oval Office. Remember, based on what we already know about women public officials and their policy orientation, the odds are that Madam President will propose and advocate policies aimed at economic equality. After all, she likely won't be a billionaire either. She likely will be a working woman who at least once in her life felt the sting of job discrimination and unequal pay. And, then, on behalf of women voters who elected her, she will launch her presidency with changes in economic policy that improve their lives.

Signs at the Women's March proclaimed WE'RE NOT BILLIONAIRE WHITE MEN because they understood these realities. They were declaring the injustice of a political system that denies them power and influence because they aren't men of means. They understood that the systemic discrimination they experience is primarily caused by the decision making of executives at the top of the workplace hierarchy, who are overwhelmingly men. They understood that America's ever-greater economic inequality engenders political inequality that in turn makes male bosses richer and women workers poorer. They were venting their frustration that few women—regardless of race or ethnicity—can do whatever they want politically whenever they want, as male billionaires and other wealthy white men with modest political experience can. They were ready to elect our first woman president.

CHAPTER 7   BUILD BRIDGES, NOT WALLS

My first professional job after graduate school was as the director of special projects for a think tank, the Institute on Pluralism and Group Identity, a subsidiary of the American Jewish Committee (AJC) and the brainchild of Irving M. Levine, a Civil Rights Movement activist. Levine and other Institute leaders were greatly concerned about the breakdown in African American–Jewish relations after the heyday of the Civil Rights Movement. The rise of the Black Power Movement had led to increasing calls for separatism between whites and blacks. Despite the movement's many successes, including passage of antidiscrimination legislation, many were still facing systemic discrimination. Levine felt that a coalition of African Americans and whites, including Jews, could continue to work to remedy this discrimination, but the new calls for separation made such collaboration difficult.

Levine's thesis, promulgated by the Institute, was that a new political coalition needed to be built among African Americans, Jews, Hispanics, and white ethnic groups, based on an idea he called "the new pluralism." His contention was that America's greatness was not built upon an amalgamation of its diverse groups into one homogeneous mass but rather upon respecting the richness of the history and culture of each of its ethnic and racial groups *and* those groups' respective "group interests," such as economic advancement unconstrained by race or ethnic discrimination. Levine believed that such respect and coalition building could yield a mutually beneficial policy agenda, such as one that addressed the common economic dislocation of members of white ethnic groups and people of color while also addressing ongoing systemic racial discrimination in policing, housing, schools, and the delivery of other public and social services.

Levine's boss, Bertram Gold, then an AJC executive vice president, stated this goal boldly in May 1972 during Richard Nixon's reelection campaign, which underscored racial and ethnic divisiveness:

> In the wake of the disillusionment over the snail's pace of social change among the nation's minorities, comes the demand for, and apparent acceptance of group rights. . . . While we oppose the concept of group rights, we see no problem with the concept of group interests. Group interests are just as real and just as legitimate as transcendent common interests.

Perhaps Gold was echoing Levine, a dreamer (though a practical one) who recognized a half century ago the problem the United States has still failed to address: the tragic separation of classes and races based on the view that one's economic security can only be achieved by preventing others from moving ahead. In other words, work for yourself or your group but not with others who differ from you or are competing with you for the same benefits. Instead, Levine postulated that respecting diversity while collaborating on common challenges would mean everyone wins.

Levine hired me in part because I had recently written a book titled *Chicago Women's Directory / Guía para las Mujeres de Chicago*, the only comprehensive bilingual women's services and political advocacy guide ever published in Chicago—a city that embodies both the pluralism Levine treasured and the racial and ethnic separation he deplored. My assignment was to build projects that furthered unity and joint advocacy among women of different communities, races, and ethnicities. We aimed to show through organizing that women of all races and economic backgrounds share a common desire for equality and opportunity.

I worked alongside author Nancy Seifer, who wrote *Absent from the Majority: Working Class Women in America*, a pamphlet published by the National Project on Ethnic America: A Depolarization Program, also an AJC project. Levine, founder and director of the project, wrote in the preface to the pamphlet that Seifer "holds out the hope for new coalitions where working class women's activism will become crucial in winning new gains for all women and in advancing social justice for all Americans."

Today's marchers and resisters seek the same. Marchers carried signs that read BUILD BRIDGES, NOT WALLS; SOMEDAY A WOMAN WILL BE PRESIDENT; and, quoting First Lady Michelle Obama, IT'S NOT ABOUT POLITICS. IT'S ABOUT BASIC HUMAN DECENCY—"it" being the goal of equality and opportunity for all women. And what better way to achieve this basic human decency than to elect a woman president, as she will understand the challenges every woman faces in a way that no president to date could?

Yet the 2016 presidential election results demonstrated that, while millions of women took Levine's fifty-year-old political agenda and Michelle Obama's words to heart and voted for Hillary Clinton—another woman who advocated basic human decency for all women, regardless of circumstance or neighborhood or ethnic background—millions of other women (most of them white and non-college-educated) did not. Instead, they chose Donald Trump, who advocated the antithesis of a basic human decency agenda and against the beliefs and policies that are at the core of the new pluralism. These millions of Trump voters were the kinds of American women Seifer wrote about. The campaign rhetoric had put women in an "us against them" scenario, pitting the winners against the losers. Clearly, more bridges need to be built.

In my graduate school studies preceding my work at the Institute, one of the books I learned the most from was *The Hidden Injuries of Class*. Authors Richard Sennett and Jonathan Cobb wove a compelling account based on their interviews in working-class Boston. They reached a conclusion they termed the "hidden injuries of class," the idea that because Americans tend to judge one another by what they do, not who they are, there can be a lack of self-respect among working-class people whose job status is low or unskilled, or people who have failed to better themselves economically while their peers have. Sennett and Cobb posited that this lack of self-respect creates bitterness and ill will, not-so-hidden injuries of classes that would be better united than divided.

Women of all kinds and all places coming together to elect our first woman president to advocate policies that help every woman could help erase these class-based hurts. A unified vote wouldn't immediately change the daily work experiences of many American women—such as the fact that working-class women like waitresses and housekeepers experience regular sexual misconduct on the job in ways that middle-class women workers do not—but it would create the context for solving this problem, perhaps starting with new federal policies that protect working women of every kind.

The fact that in 2018 all twenty-two US women senators, Republicans along with Democrats, came together—dare I say, built a bridge to stand on together—to advocate policies eliminating sexual harassment in congressional offices shows the willingness and capacity of women working together. These women, like the women they represent, come from vastly different backgrounds and have differing group interests, but they built that bridge and stood as one.

Coalitions like these can help ameliorate the injuries that Sennett and Cobb discussed, for every woman suffers the first injury of class—that is, being second-class because she is a woman. In *Absent from the Majority*, Seifer quotes a woman interviewed for an article in the *Annals of the American Academy of Political and Social Sciences*: "I think that women's liberation has got to be the kind of group that is willing to go out and educate the husbands and men, and it's got to be involving people like me and the things that are really important to us, like if we've got to work, a job where we can earn a decent salary, or women living alone should be able to support their own families." Exactly. Let's build more bridges and stand on them together.

In a review of *Strangers in Their Own Land: Anger and Mourning on the American Right* by Arlie Russell Hochschild, Robert Kuttner of the *American Prospect* wrote: "If the government had been doing its job, their homes would not have been turned into a ruined landscape of toxic waste." He was referring to the environmental degradation of southwest Louisiana. However, thinking nationally and metaphorically, "a ruined landscape of toxic waste" describes tens of thousands of other American communities populated by women of various group interests suffering from the notion that it is us against them when really, it is billionaire (and otherwise wealthy) white men against the rest of us. Irving M. Levine said fifty years ago that us against them wouldn't work, and today we know it hasn't (just consider the economic dislocation and the resulting stagnation of family income found throughout the United States today). Organizing a campaign to elect a woman president would acknowledge this ruined, toxic landscape of women's lives and identify common interests and a shared policy agenda across groups of women, forming the basis for building bridges on which we can all stand together.

CHAPTER 8

DEAR TRUMP: YOU GOT 99 PROBLEMS AND THIS BITCH IS 1

Historically, *bitch* has been used to demean a woman who is assertive about what she wants, unconcerned with—in fact, hostile to—the traditional notions of femininity that hobble women. She is a woman who, for instance, asserts the right of American women to the presidency and the importance of overcoming centuries of precedent to elect one. She is a "nasty woman," the label Donald Trump used to describe Hillary Clinton during their third presidential debate in 2016.

Several posters at the Women's March displayed the expression "nasty woman," and some included vagina imagery, along with statements like KEEP YOUR ROSARIES OFF MY OVARIES and NO UTERUS, NO OPINION. Using imagery of women's anatomy to make nasty-woman assertions of women's rights, the marchers also reclaimed the word *bitch*, using it not as a demeaning insult but as motivational shorthand for an assertive, independent woman who takes actions like electing a woman president.

Some of us marchers (of the "bitch" ilk as described above) had never used the word *bitch* to describe our feminist self-concept. Frankly, many of us were uncomfortable with it. The word felt pejorative, given its typical usage. In our campaign to be respected and convincing about our women's rights agenda and campaigns, using shorthand that is generally used by men as a belittling description of women didn't feel like a smart idea. However, a turning point for me was when I read a *Vox* article in which Hillary Clinton repeated something Facebook COO Sheryl Sandberg told her before the 2016 presidential campaign: "When a woman advocates for others, she tends to be well-liked. The moment she starts advocating for herself, people tend to turn against her." What was that about being a bitch? As one Women's March poster stated, quoting Madonna: I'M TOUGH, I'M AMBITIOUS, AND I KNOW EXACTLY WHAT I WANT. IF THAT MAKES ME A BITCH, SO BE IT. *So be it for me, and so be it for us, too.*

I've since come to advocate this marcher's expression of women's confidence and rebellion against the status quo. I have also watched and heard hip-hop's self-styled feminist stars, such as Beyoncé and Nicki Minaj, use the word *bitch* to describe attitudes I now share with them. "When I am assertive, I'm a bitch," Minaj said in the MTV documentary *My Time Now*. "When a man is assertive, he's a boss. He bossed up. No negative connotation behind 'bossed up.' But lots of negative connotation behind being a 'bitch.'"

Let's just go ahead and claim the word *bitch* to describe our attitude about electing our first woman president. I think we have to in order to clarify our willingness to be "bitchy"—that is, forceful and demanding. Because let's face it: that's what electing our first American woman president will require.

In my research for this book, I found a Pinterest site called "BITCH, I GOT THIS (Confidence)." Yes, let's use the word *bitch* to tell the world we have the confidence to take care of our highest-priority business, electing a woman president. As one Women's March poster read, BITCHES GET STUFF DONE. We have only to get to work to get this stuff done. We have the numbers. According to CAWP:

- Women outnumber men among registered voters.
- Women turn out to vote at rates that equal or exceed men's rates.
- A higher proportion of women than men vote among US citizens age 18 to 64.
- For eight consecutive presidential elections, more women have voted than men.

> I'm **TOUGH,** I'm AMBITIOUS, and I KNOW **EXACTLY** what I want. If that makes me a **BITCH, OKAY.**
>
> —Madonna

Further, millennials are projected to surpass baby boomers as the country's largest living adult generation in 2019. Combined with Generation X, they already make up a bigger voting bloc than baby boomers and the silent generation, and according to a survey by *Vanity Fair*, "millennial women are more politically engaged than they have been in years, with an unparalleled capacity to effect change."

We have the voters and we also have the candidates. As I write this book, four women, all Democratic US senators—Kirsten Gillibrand, Kamala Harris, Elizabeth Warren, and Amy Klobuchar—are presumed to be considering a presidential run in 2020. All four have core legislative, personal, and political strengths, making each a viable candidate, but they won't all survive the run-up—each will have to convince the rest of us, "Bitch, I got this."

This number of potential women candidates is a first in American history, and getting one of them elected might not be

Millennial women are more likely than the general population to support activist campaigns.

just a fantasy, according to *Politico Magazine* contributing editor Bill Scher. For one thing, almost 60 percent of the 2016 Democratic presidential primary electorate were women, many of whom are still ready for change. For another, Democrats who self-identify as "social liberals" make up the majority (53 percent) of Democrats, and according to Scher, these voters have "grown accustomed to breaking barriers and won't readily accept a coldly pessimistic argument that running another woman against Trump would be a bad idea." Echoing suffragist Carrie Chapman Catt's 1916 battle cry, Scher added, "the woman's hour must again strike."

Notwithstanding these positive trends and the individual strengths of all four potential candidates, Scher concluded by saying that "she won't become a superstar by anointment, as Obama was in 2004. She will have to make it happen by breaking out of the Senate procedural muck, delivering soaring speeches, crafting signature policy ideas, picking high-profile fights, outwitting conservatives and proving she knows how to triumph over the inevitable misogynistic attacks." This is where the rest of us come in to help our prospective Madam President get it done.

Scher's description of the voters most likely to support Gillibrand, Harris, Warren, or Klobuchar sounds a lot like women who say, "I'm tough, I'm ambitious, and I know what I want. If that makes me a bitch, so be it." No problem. We got this.

In the past, one of the main ways ambitious American women politicians tried to soften their assertive presence and justify their entry into the public square was by using the rationale that women are purer than men. Women are incorruptible, women are selfless, women aren't interested in power, women just want to make the world a better place. So, men, you have nothing to fear from our desire for political power—our ambition isn't really about that. It's about doing good, always selflessly and politely.

That rationale is now history. "This bitch is 1" ("this bitch" being our first woman president) is our new rallying cry. Get with the program, my old-school girlfriends.

Estoy aquí con
LA FUERZA
de MILES de
personas. NO
me SUBESTIME
B.O.
Heretostay!
Same pencils
Same exams
Hear us holler
Same scores
Same careers
78 cents to
his dollar

CHAPTER 9

HEAR US HOLLER

A young woman marcher proclaimed on her sign ESTOY AQUÍ CON LA FUERZA DE MILES DE PERSONAS. NO ME SUBESTIMES. HERE TO STAY! B.O. (referencing Barack Obama). Translation: "I am here with the force of thousands of people. Do not underestimate me." Another woman's sign read SAME PENCILS. SAME EXAMS. HEAR US HOLLER. SAME SCORES. SAME CAREERS. 78 CENTS TO HIS DOLLAR. Her last statement is a point well worth repeating!

When I think about hollering or speaking as loudly and forcefully as possible—in this case, about electing our first woman president—I think about all of the fearless women I have read about who serve as courageous examples of women leading. Happily, of late, there are a lot more of them to read about and admire than there used to be. Fearless women are experiencing a moment in the marches they organize, the speeches they give, the actions they take, and the political campaigns they launch—so often against great odds. This moment is also being celebrated in the publication of many new books for both women and girls, often presented in formats that celebrate these women with strong images and vibrant colors. I love paging through them, and I can't seem to resist buying them, especially those for girls and teenagers.

My favorite of these new books so far is from the Real Lives series, called *Fearless Women: Courageous Females Who Refused to Be Denied.* I love everything about it, from the title to the colors to the selection of women portrayed. Affirming my Chicago pride, I cheered for the appearance of two Chicago-rooted heroines of mine on consecutive pages: the justly famous Jane Addams, whose fearless life story I shared in chapter 4, and the unjustly unfamous guitarist and gospel singer Sister Rosetta Tharpe, who was an inspiration to Elvis Presley and many other rock-and-roll stars. After reading those two pages, I returned to the book's table of contents and saw that the authors had moved beyond the tried-and-true famous and fearless to highlight the noteworthy but obscure. I previously had heard of just seventeen of the fifty-four women included in the book!

Chelsea Clinton did the same in her book *She Persisted: 13 American Women Who Changed the World.* Its title was inspired by Senator Elizabeth Warren, who spoke against the 2017 confirmation of Attorney General Jeff Sessions, only to be interrupted and then silenced by Senate Majority Leader Mitch McConnell. Later, during remarks following the confirmation vote, McConnell said that Warren "was giving a lengthy speech. She had appeared to violate the rule. She was warned. She was given an explanation. Nevertheless, she persisted." These words were immediately adopted by women's rights activists, sparking the #ShePersisted movement, which champions women who keep working to break down barriers, despite being silenced or ignored.

In her book, Clinton celebrates heroic women such as Clara Lemlich, a labor organizer; Claudette Colvin, a teenager in Montgomery, Alabama, who refused to give up her seat on a bus months before Rosa Parks did the same; and Virginia Apgar, a doctor who created the Apgar score to measure newborn babies' health. Though these women are unknown to too many of us, they share a legacy of accomplishment that could justifiably be celebrated in a hundred more books. Whether famous or newly recognized, these women refused to be denied their right to be heard, and the lesson from their stories is clear: holler loudly about what is to be done, and then work hard to get it done.

So I read, and read again, the biographies of unheralded women who have made our world better. I think about who these women were beyond their now-celebrated public lives. I think about the paths they chose moving from obscurity to recognition. What forks in the road did they encounter along the way? How did they decide which one to take? How did they sustain their courage to holler?

For some of these answers, I turn to women who I've heard holler. During my political organizing career, I have worked alongside dozens of them. Like so many other accomplished women, most were born into ordinary families. Perhaps no one in their families had hollered before they did. Most will likely remain unknown. But no matter. It is the significance of their speech and their accomplishments—changing women's lives for the better—that matters.

Every woman we can learn from, we should learn from. We are about to elect a woman president, and as any savvy political or community organizer would instruct, sharing other women's stories motivates action. Here are the instructive, hollering stories of three women from my political organizing life. They are Gale Cincotta, Nancy Jefferson, and Sol Flores. All three grew up in Chicago, home to too many unsung feminist heroines.

Cincotta, now deceased, was a community activist who fought redlining, an invidious banking practice in racially changing neighborhoods that discriminatorily inhibits minority homeowners from obtaining a mortgage. I worked with her early in my career when I was the lead organizer and spokesperson for a coalition of organizations lobbying for legislation to improve the lives of Illinois women, including the Equal Rights Amendment (the still-not-ratified constitutional amendment that would explicitly guarantee equal rights to all citizens, regardless of sex), as well as measures to advance women's economic status. I recruited Cincotta to be a spokesperson for a constituency of women often assumed not to be part of women's movement activities: the blue- and pink-collar women of Chicago's ethnic neighborhoods. She was inspiring in every way imaginable.

Jefferson, also now deceased, lived in a predominately black neighborhood and spent her life countering the notion that she and her neighbors had "no control over their lives," according to a student who interviewed her. "She attacked the institutions that perpetuated that [notion] with a vengeance," he said. I worked closely with Jefferson on the 1982–1983 campaign to elect the first African American mayor of Chicago, Harold Washington. Jefferson, along with other African American Chicagoans, considered that political campaign to be akin to the Civil Rights Movement because it crystalized the fight for the causes they, often led by Jefferson, had always championed—equal opportunity in every domain of life, including housing, education, and jobs—decades after the Great Migration to Chicago began.

For over fifteen years, Flores, a former student of mine, has led an organization that helps homeless Hispanic youth better their lives. In 2017, Flores jumped into the 2018 Illinois Democratic primary to run for the US House of Representatives when her district's incumbent announced he was stepping down and simultaneously endorsed a male colleague. She hollered throughout the campaign about the importance of women running for office and her commitment to creating policy solutions to significant problems facing women and girls, such as sexual assault. Flores lost the race, but her courage in telling her own story was a momentous victory. "[It] reflects another shift in strategy where women candidates embrace their experiences and perspectives *as women* as an electoral asset, instead of treating their gender as a hurdle to overcome on the campaign trail," Kelly Dittmar, a CAWP scholar, wrote. Talk about hollering!

If we were to ask Cincotta, Jefferson, or Flores why they led fights for justice, each would tell you that her fight began with outrage at an injustice that necessitated hollering about its wrongheadedness. Hollering begat action that mitigated injustice, and persistence yielded the defeat of powerful enemies. When faced with the worst obstacles, these women hollered back, knowing that even the worst can usually be overcome, even if it might take a while.

Every woman can stand up and say, "Hear us holler!" Maybe once you holler, you'll become famous. Maybe you won't. But you will be heard. And in being heard, you will matter, regardless of how small your circle is. Hear me out on this one: when I began my political organizing career, I learned about the power of hollering in small groups. For instance, the collective that wrote the *Chicago Women's Directory / Guía para las Mujeres de Chicago* included just seven women. But look at the impact we had—we published in Spanish as well as English, and we reached women all over the city, in part through free distribution of the book, which we underwrote ourselves. With the rise of the internet, virtually every woman now has her very own worldwide printing press, which she can use when hollering about electing our first woman president.

Of course, Cincotta, Jefferson, and Flores would likely remind us that there is power and righteousness (and safety) in our large movement. Think about the wise marcher who proclaimed I AM HERE WITH THE FORCE OF THOUSANDS OF PEOPLE. DO NOT UNDERESTIMATE ME. Listening to my friends who holler, I hear this righteousness, untempered by fear because they are doing the right thing. You can, too.

However, remember this important truth as you holler: maybe, despite all your hollering, our first woman president won't do everything you want her to do. Maybe she will endorse some policies that you don't like or that you think are bad for women. Maybe she will accept money from corporations you don't like or from individuals who are anti-feminist. Maybe she will say she is not a feminist—that she is not a woman president but just a president. No matter: she will be *our woman president* because *we* hollered *for her*. For what is a greater reason to holler than to eliminate the inequality that electing her will begin to end? It's time to say to the world: hear us holler!

> Hollering begat action that mitigated injustice, and persistence yielded the defeat of powerful enemies. When faced with the worst obstacles, these women hollered back, knowing that even the worst can usually be overcome, even if it might take a while.

CHAPTER 10

BEYONCÉ RUNS THE WORLD

By now, there is probably not a woman alive who doesn't know of Beyoncé or, for that matter, her songs "Run the World (Girls)" and "Formation." I believe this is because Beyoncé unapologetically asserts for women everywhere—via pop songs that every woman can relate to and understand—that every woman has the right to be in charge. This is why Beyoncé's songs have become feminist anthems and why her lyrics have become rallying cries to defeat Donald Trump and elect a woman president.

At the 2017 Chicago Women's March, this queen of pop music (and now of feminist politics) was everywhere. As I read and photographed the posters proclaiming that women run the world and advising us to get in formation, I realized that the best pop music serves as a call to arms that reaches across our diverse backgrounds. And we need that. It becomes the theme music for building bridges, not walls, and, in the case of *this* call to arms, it becomes the anthem for those electing our first woman president. Marchers knew this; they quoted Beyoncé's anthems often.

The rhetorical power of these two favorite Beyoncé anthems rests in their combination of lyrics and music: with a compelling beat and powerful phrasing, they are easily remembered and internalized. In the case of "Run the World" ("Who are we? / What we brought? / The world (who run this motha', yeah)"), there is no doubt about the song's statement and purpose. The song opens with "Girls, we run this motha', yeah" four times, followed by "Who run the world? Girls!" repeated four times. Lest there be any doubt about her music's meaning, at the 2014 MTV Video Music Awards ceremony, Beyoncé sang in front of a big banner that read FEMINIST. A few years later in 2018, I heard a spontaneous outburst of "Run the World (Girls)" at the Women's March in New York City.

It's important to note that neither Beyoncé nor the marchers are claiming a right to personal empowerment when they sing "Run the World (Girls)." Nor are they celebrating some kind of *self*-actualization or *personal* spiritual awakening (Beyoncé appears to already have all that!). Instead, unified in song, they are celebrating the right to systemic political power for women, for us "girls."

This claim of the right to run the world embodies the case made here that a woman should be POTUS. Beyoncé advocates women running the world: that's what POTUS does.

In proclaiming the possibility of feminists running the world, Beyoncé is also pointing to the possibility—and hope—that every woman will get in formation to claim *her* power to run the world by, oh, say, electing Madam President. OKAY LADIES, LET'S GET IN FORMATION! read one poster carried by a young black woman. That's why women were marching in the first place: to get in formation to protest the defeat of the woman who should have been our first woman president.

When you listen to Beyoncé's 2016 song "Formation," you will notice that she explicitly sings about her power to create high-achieving men: "You just might be a black Bill Gates in the making, 'cause I slay." She asserts the kind of power Madam President would have—the power to tell men not only what to do (*she* is the executive, not them) but also how to become high achievers on behalf of themselves and the women in their lives. Beyoncé also describes herself as a woman who has "hot sauce in [her] bag," recalling Hillary Clinton's remark about Tabasco sauce, which preceded "Formation" by four years. (*Condé Nast Traveler* asked Clinton's office in 2012 what she always packed.

A staffer responded that she keeps a "small mesh bag filled with the basics . . . and a mini bottle of Tabasco Sauce for adding spice to her meals.") I don't think Beyoncé's lyric was a coincidence.

Tragically, in the 2016 presidential campaign, too many white women failed to get in formation with African American women for Clinton to win. However, the data on their voting are instructive for our formation of the next campaign of a would-be Madam President: marginal swings by *white women voters who are Beyoncé fans*, joining *African American women who are Beyoncé fans* in such key states as Ohio, Michigan, Florida, and Pennsylvania, could mean a win. Beyoncé's guidance is clear: connect the relevant pop culture message to the deeply felt and common concerns of every woman. Get in formation for, say, equal pay.

Pop culture references by political candidates have a long history in this country because such references help connect the candidate to the voters, who may then think of the candidate more favorably because they like the reference. The poem that became "The Star-Spangled Banner" was written to bring the nation together during the War of 1812. That song *still* rallies political action more than two hundred years later: some stand and salute because of their belief in the ideas the song expresses, others kneel in protest because those ideas don't reflect their life experience—in either case, the song mobilizes political action.

A friend recently told me, as several others have, that she voted for Hillary Clinton despite her dismay about Clinton's email server use while serving as the US secretary of state and her decision to remain married to a philanderer. But then came the punch line: "I didn't realize until after Election Day how much I wanted a woman president." My friend was endorsing Beyoncé's declaration of independence for every woman, for women's right to the presidency—a right not abrogated by the occasional bad judgment or misstep. This is the same right that male presidential candidates have. To put this in perspective, just think about Donald Trump's bad judgments. As I said earlier, women leaders don't have to be perfect; they should, just as men should, do what's right.

Today, as we again make the case for electing a woman president and see various women consider becoming candidates, there are numerous songs to add to the Madam President campaign playlist. "You Don't Own Me" by Lesley Gore, a favorite women's empowerment anthem since it hit the Billboard Hot 100 in 1964, was big in President Obama's 2012 reelection campaign (to highlight his pro-women policies) and could be big again. Consider these lyrics:

> And don't tell me what to do
> Don't tell me what to say . . .
> I'm free and I love to be free
> To live my life the way I want
> To say and do whatever I please

This includes becoming president. Even though I first heard "You Don't Own Me" as a young woman, I can still sing every note and say every word. No wonder smart campaign strategists landed on it!

But Lesley Gore's anthem isn't the only one. There are other songs that celebrate and affirm women's autonomy and fitness for taking charge. From Aretha Franklin's "Respect" to Dolly Parton's "Working Girl" to Taylor Swift's "Shake It Off" to various, albeit salacious, Nicki Minaj declarations, there are anthems aplenty to motivate and inspire.

And, when things go (momentarily) south, as Madam President's campaign inevitably will, consider my all-time favorite get-up-and-go song, "Lord Don't Move the Mountain," written by Doris Akers. It begins: "Now Lord don't move my mountain / But give me the strength to climb." It has been recorded by Mahalia Jackson, Etta James, and, in my favorite version, Inez Andrews. Here are the words that get me every time:

> Now Lord don't move my mountain
> But give me the strength to climb
> And Lord, don't take away my stumbling blocks
> But lead me all around

I am not a religious person, but I am a spiritual one, and I believe you must have a spiritual side if you're going to be a woman who elects our first woman president. Time to get in formation.

CHAPTER 11
FLAG DAY

Less than a year after the Declaration of Independence was signed, the United States adopted the stars and stripes as its national flag. While the official National Flag Day holiday was not established by Congress until 1946, the practice of celebrating the flag as a symbol of the nation has been with us since the flag's adoption.

Too often in our nation's history, flag imagery has been appropriated by partisans of political beliefs that are detrimental to women. This was egregiously evident in Donald Trump's 2016 presidential campaign, which featured all kinds of merchandise and signage showing the American flag while Trump himself spouted hateful speech against women, racial minorities, Muslims, and people with disabilities. The flag-waving conservatives who backed Trump advocated policies that would strip away women's hard-won rights—the very values that the flag represents.

No more, if we have anything to do with it!

For our campaign to elect our first woman president, we must reclaim this imagery, even if some of us understandably kneel when they see the flag. We need to prove that the flag is for everyone because of what it represents: the idea of liberty and justice for all, including in the Oval Office. In the 98 years since American women won suffrage, we have been active

> The flag represents our rights, too. It belongs to women and those who seek justice for women, not just to those who would appropriate Nazi slogans and beliefs and attempt to validate them with flag imagery.

participants in our political system. Yet our right to equality has not always been recognized and our interests not always represented. We need to remind the country that the flag represents our rights, too.

Millions of marchers agreed. American flag imagery and accompanying messages were prominent at every US Women's March I've seen pictured. At the 2017 Chicago Women's March, I saw flag imagery on signs, clothes, buildings, light poles, and fences. Its intention was clear: to make the point that the flag belongs to women and those who seek justice for women, not just to those who would appropriate Nazi slogans and beliefs and attempt to validate them with flag imagery.

I am the daughter of an immigrant. My mother and her parents escaped Austria in the face of the Nazis. I am also the daughter of a Jewish American father who, while a pacifist, enlisted to fight in World War II because of the threat of Nazism and what it would mean for the United States if Hitler prevailed. Once, when my father and I were discussing his decision to become a soldier, he told me he had known at the time about the America First Committee, which was founded in 1940 to oppose US intervention in World War II (even though the Nazis had by then invaded Poland and were attacking other parts of Europe) and then was disbanded after the Japanese attacked Pearl Harbor and the United States entered the war.

I imagine one reason my father knew about the committee was because of the anti-Semitism of some of its leaders. One was Charles Lindbergh, the famous aviator, who said, "Instead of agitating for war, the Jewish groups in this country should be opposing it in every possible way for they will be among the first to feel its consequences. Tolerance is a virtue that depends upon peace and strength. History shows that it cannot survive war and devastation. A few far-sighted Jewish people realize this and stand opposed to intervention. But the majority still do not."

President Franklin D. Roosevelt publicly dismissed these views, and millions of young men who believed in liberty and justice for all—including my father and father-in-law—enlisted. We are fortunate they did.

In 1999, Donald Trump called Republican presidential candidate Pat Buchanan a "Hitler lover" after Buchanan said Hitler initially wasn't a major threat to the United States in World War II. But then, years later, there was Trump giving his inaugural address, repeating the phrase of Nazi appeasers: "From this day forward, it's going to be only, 'America First.'"

I say it is time to take back the flag from today's America Firsters, from these disbelievers in liberty and justice for all. It is time for women to declare their independence from the second-class citizenship that leaves them foreclosed from executive governmental power. It is time for us to elect the first American woman president, one who will establish justice for all.

We can accomplish this by telling stories about patriotic women's lives and deeds. We can tell stories of women's political leadership that have advanced the common good. Remember, that's what the campaign to elect the first American woman president needs to prove: that electing a woman president will yield a greater common good, for she will advance opportunities for women and girls, thereby advancing justice for all.

When I think about how much has changed in my lifetime to make the election of a woman president more plausible, I am hopeful. As a girl, I pledged allegiance every day in school to a flag that represented "liberty and justice for all." Yet, when my family traveled south, we saw separate water fountains for whites and blacks. As a teenager, I was told that because I was Jewish, I wouldn't be able to visit a friend at her parent's vacation home. As a young woman, I was married before the US Supreme Court's 1973 *Roe v. Wade* decision, overruling those who said women don't have the right to control their own reproductive destiny by having access to legal abortion. In the subsequent decades, all Americans have made great gains, regardless of their race, religion, or gender. Now it's time to take the next step.

The marchers who used flag imagery were onto something big. Those of us who will elect America's first woman president are Americans, too. No one is first; all of us stand together as equals. The flag symbolizes this truth. And so will Madam President. Let's make every day of our campaign Flag Day.

CHAPTER 12

HISTORY HAS ITS EYES ON ALL OF US

The idea that history has its eyes on us could feel oppressive. Might we fail to make the world a better place? Might we dismiss too blithely the harm being done to humanity, including by men who regularly abuse their executive power? Is forbearance ever enough in the face of injustice and women's inequality?

I think not. Millions of marchers and those who are part of the #MeToo and #ShePersisted movements think not. The suffragists would think not. I sense they are watching our next steps and entreating us to fight for justice and equality. I sense their telling us, "Do what we did. Remember that marching is just the first step. We marched, and we won women the vote. You marched. Now, you can win women the presidency."

Yes, the American suffragists' march to victory was slow. There were almost seventy-five years between the Declaration of Sentiments, the suffragists' declaration of American women's independence, and the ratification of the Nineteenth Amendment. After that, it wasn't until the Voting Rights Act of 1965, when race discrimination in voting was federally prohibited, that legal barriers preventing African Americans from exercising their voting rights under the Fifteenth Amendment were overcome.

> It's been almost two hundred years since the suffragists started their campaign for equality, and women currently represent only 23 percent of the Senate and 19.3 percent of the House—and there has never been a woman president.

As I've shared with you, it took well into the twentieth century for women to gain even a toehold in public office. For instance, it wasn't until 1985 that women made up 5 percent of the US Congress and not until 1992—the original "Year of the Woman"—that four women served in the US Senate. It then took another twenty-four years after that for a woman to be a major-party candidate for the US presidency. The suffragists are watching us to see how much further American women travel on the road to equality. Let's not disappoint them.

I understand how a person could fairly conclude that woman-by-woman advancement strategies, such as "leaning in"—the strategy coined by Facebook COO Sheryl Sandberg in her 2013 book on women's advancement—haven't amounted to much. We have only to examine the woeful data I've already shared to confirm this. Now, after the 2016 presidential election debacle, it's time to recognize that history is expecting many of us to renew and deepen our commitment to *collective* political action. The ultimate expression of this commitment will be our successful partnership in the campaign to elect Madam President.

An inspiring poster at the 2017 Chicago Women's March read I AM NOT FREE WHILE ANY WOMAN IS UNFREE, making it clear that it is every woman's duty to work for all women to be created equal. American history resonates with stories of women who made the world better for womankind. Often, this history occurred in the most unlikely of places, under the most unlikely of conditions, by the most unlikely of women, proving that any woman can play a role in freeing other women.

I met a young woman health care worker from Joliet, Illinois, at a Planned

Parenthood breakfast held before the 2017 Chicago Women's March. Just a week earlier, she had attended a union rally, where she learned about the Women's March. She had driven to Chicago early that Saturday morning alone because her friends had to work. She told me, however, that traveling and marching alone didn't matter to her—she was on a mission to make a difference. When I introduced her to one of the Planned Parenthood staff members, she volunteered: "Whatever I can do to continue to make a difference, just let me know what that is and where to show up."

After that Women's March, I took an Amtrak train to my home in southwest Michigan. When the train conductor saw my Women's March button, she told me how sorry she was to have to work and miss the March. She also told me that many of her friends had traveled 200 miles from their homes in Battle Creek, Michigan, to the March in Chicago to make *her-story*. Making herstory means getting up early and traveling however far is necessary to do our part and fulfill our duty to ourselves and each other. Those women from Battle Creek knew this. They knew history has its eyes on all of us.

When I feel the weight of history's expectations, I think about two herstory-making friends who—no matter what—persisted: Addie L. Wyatt and Florence Scala. Both were born about a century ago, and both were committed to fighting for women's political power and equality. I met them when I was in my twenties, around the time when *Unbought and Unbossed*, Shirley Chisholm's autobiography, had become my bible. I remember thinking that if Chisholm, Wyatt, and Scala could be unbought and unbossed, if they could rise up when they were pushed down, why, then so could I.

Addie L. Wyatt was born in an African American community in rural Mississippi. She was the eldest daughter of a family of eight children that moved to Chicago as part of the Great Migration. In 1941, when she was just seventeen years old and already the mother of two sons, she applied to be a typist at Armour and Company, a Chicago-based meatpacking plant. However, because the position was open to white women only, she had to take a job on the assembly line instead. By 1954, she had risen to become the first woman president of a local chapter of the United Packinghouse Workers of America. While working *and* representing herself and her coworkers, Wyatt participated in the 1963 March on Washington and marched from Selma to Montgomery, Alabama, in 1965. She also was a volunteer organizer for Dr. Martin Luther King Jr.'s Southern Christian Leadership Conference (SCLC), an association of local groups of primarily African American activists committed to using nonviolent action to promote civil rights in the South.

I met Wyatt in the mid-1970s when we worked together on the campaign to ratify the Equal Rights Amendment. By that time, she had served with Eleanor Roosevelt on President John F. Kennedy's Commission on the Status of Women and she had cofounded the Coalition of Labor Union Women, the National Organization for Women, and Operation Breadbasket, an outgrowth of the SCLC committed to improving the economic lives of African Americans.

Born to Italian immigrants on Chicago's Near West Side, Florence Scala became an activist as a young woman by partnering with Hull-House, the center of community organizing and feminist causes near her family's apartment. She led the fight against Chicago Mayor Richard J. Daley after he announced in 1961 that he wanted to level the neighborhood, including Hull-House, to build a campus for the University of Illinois at Chicago (UIC). Chicago author and historian Studs Terkel opened his great book *Division Street: America* with Scala's story and described her as his heroine. "She tried with intelligence and courage to save the soul of our city," he said, in Scala's *Chicago Tribune* obituary.

The original Hull-House building and one other *were* saved, but much of the rest of the neighborhood was razed. While I was studying the history of American women political leaders at UIC, I gave tours of the buildings, which had become a museum run by the university. It was in that capacity that I met Scala, who told me many stories of her fight to save her neighborhood.

Covering one of Scala's protests at the mayor's office, the *Chicago Tribune* reported that Scala said the mayor was "going to understand what it is like to live in a real democracy." In a real democracy, women are involved in every level of government, and they sit in every chair.

Indeed, marching is just the first step because history has its eyes on us. The women who came before and fought for our rights and our freedoms need us to step up and out *now*.

MARCHING is just the FIRST STEP SO WEAR COMFORTABLE SHOES!

PART TWO

Advocacy on behalf of women's rights has been my life's work. My first campaign was as a college student, working to convince my college to provide birth control at its campus health clinic. When the other organizers of this effort and I started out, several of us had recently read *Sisterhood Is Powerful: An Anthology of Writings from the Women's Liberation Movement*. The book motivated us to fight against injustices like the disparate treatment at the college's health clinic. As it turned out, our strategy—identifying a common goal and acting in concert to achieve it—worked. We were *done being quiet* about discriminatory and short-sighted college policy.

Who knew that we could convince the college's board of trustees and president to even hear us, much less change their egregious policy? But we persisted, recruiting hundreds of supporters, and we won the change we sought. We organized our campaign, action by action, so that every participant could play a meaningful role both through her own individual actions and through her participation in the collective outcry and mobilization.

In the following chapters, I name and describe the actions we took then that you can take now in the campaign to elect our first woman president, now that you're done being quiet, too! To do so, I share more herstory and accounts of women's political valor, as well as my ideas about the importance and value of the actions I propose. Each chapter focuses on a specific action, its theme drawn from language on Women's March posters. Think of these actions the same way you think of your daily action plan at your job or the plans you make with your family and friends. Likewise, these political actions aren't haphazard. *You* are the decision maker for the choices reflected in your action plan. For instance, *you* will decide when and where to speak about the importance of electing our first woman president and when and how to become actively involved in her campaign.

Your mission in taking these actions is to:

- Commit to regular personal efforts to help elect Madam President, both by working for her and by being a political voice.
- Mobilize every woman you possibly can to make this same commitment as an instigator of our American revolution.

You don't need to take every action at once. I recommend you begin with the action that matters most to you. Then, build your political presence while working in concert with other women—the best way to get this job done! Think about your action plan in this light: the more politically influential you

> As you carry out this mission, what matters most is your steadfast commitment to act. Revolutions don't happen overnight, and every day presents a new chance to act, to share messages that resonate, and to model behavior that will mobilize other women.

become, the more you will be able to do and the better able you will be to convince others to elect our first woman president.

As you carry out this mission, what matters most is your steadfast commitment to act. Revolutions don't happen overnight, and every day presents a new chance to act, to share messages that resonate, and to model behavior that will mobilize other women (for instance, marching and then marching again).

At the same time, a main truth of politics is that while political campaigns have strategists (and the bigger the campaign, the more likely those strategists are to be well-paid men) and staffers to carry out their campaign strategy, that staff is dependent on volunteers to undertake much of the day-to-day work to realize the campaign's goals. This means that while strategists are evaluating demographic data about potential voters, volunteers are canvassing the precincts the strategists have selected, texting and calling likely participants in house meetings or fund-raising parties, organizing events for voters to hear more about the candidate, or getting voters to the polls.

In the #ShePersisted, #TimesUp, and #MeToo era, the power of every woman to make a significant difference in politics is manifest as it never has been before in our nation's history. For evidence of this, one needs only to recall the cascade of individual women who brought charges against abusive men, toppling them and spurring beneficial policy changes. As a result, we are now positioned to win our next revolution: electing our first woman president, who will prove that *this* executive power is the domain of women, too.

This revolution won't be easy, or pretty, or nice. But no revolution ever is. Our outrage that an unqualified man who boasted of sexual assault would beat a superbly qualified and polite woman for the presidency means "No more nice girls," as early feminist writer Ellen Willis put it. Forget turning a blind eye. Forget nicely insisting. Forget being polite. Forget wearing the white suits, hoping imagery will sufficiently motivate. We now know #TimesUp for all that.

There is no wrong way to be a woman; that's the case to make.

Early in my life as a political activist, I read Saul Alinsky's *Reveille for Radicals*, a step-by-step handbook for social justice organizers. On the title page was a quote from philosopher Thomas Paine, whose writings inspired the Declaration of Independence and the American Revolution, and who inspired Saul Alinsky's social justice organizing. Paine's statement, written in response to the idea of swearing allegiance to the King of England, read: "Let them call me rebel and welcome, I feel no concern from it; but I should suffer the misery of devils, were I to make a whore of my soul." Alinsky believed that to act contrary to one's self-interest, as Paine advised against, in his case to swearing allegiance to the King of England—in our case, to not work for the election of a woman president if you are a woman—is the equivalent of selling one's soul. Strong words, to be sure, but strong words mobilize successful revolutions.

As we work to elect Madam President, we should, as Alinsky also recommended, act with "cool anger and conscious understanding based on experience...[and not] confuse power patterns with the personalities of the individuals involved; in other words, to hate conditions, not individuals." The power pattern in question here is men's power over women, the condition worthy of hatred is that no American woman has ever been elected president. The chapters that follow describe the ways to fight these conditions—what Alinsky called "actions far more calculated, deliberate, directive, and effective."

As you undertake these actions, please don't get distracted or discouraged by all the challenges we faced the last time we campaigned to elect Madam President. If you're like me, thinking about them will just give you a big fat headache. Besides, by now, revisiting the challenges Hillary Clinton faced and her partisans had to address (the same ones that future women presidential candidates likely will face) is beside the main point. Given what's going on

SOMETIMES IT TAKES balls TO bE A WOMAN

these days, we don't have time to talk about modulating our voices, or changing what we wear, or rebutting questions about whether women have sufficient stamina, or considering whether we need to act like men (oh, right, only sometimes). Also—and this is an important cautionary note—we should not get trapped in inaction by the fact that "party trumps gender in guiding vote choice," or more significantly, that being a Democrat or a Republican or an independent is more important than being a woman. Electing our first woman president is a singularly important campaign *for every woman*, regardless of temporal political party preference.

This is the case to make, relentlessly, as you undertake the actions I propose here: unite, name the enemy, speak, connect, resist, fight, believe, educate, write, litigate, and elect yourself. They will vary in sequence as circumstances dictate. They will require varying levels of commitment along the way. They will need to be repeated many times as we work to elect Madam President. But they will always matter. **Let's get going.**

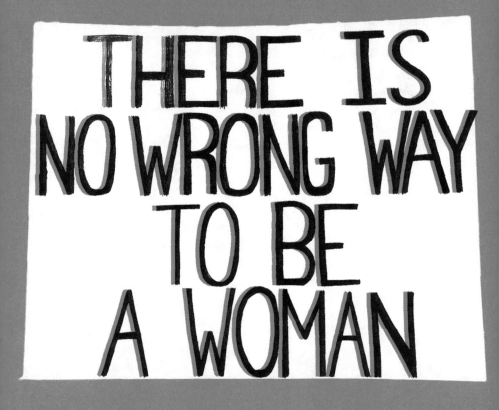

CHAPTER 13

THERE IS NO WRONG WAY TO BE A WOMAN

ACTION: UNITE

We start this action plan by affirming that, as one sign at the Women's March read, THERE IS NO WRONG WAY TO BE A WOMAN. We cannot win if we don't share the belief that we are all equal, however different we may appear on the surface or in our policy positions. It's time to find our common ground so that we can elect a woman president who betters our world.

A Women's March sign carried by a young woman with pink hair read 65,853,516 STRONG. This is the number of voters in the 2016 presidential election—the majority by more than two million—who voted to elect Hillary Clinton. As everyone knows, if not for the archaic Electoral College system (as arcane as the constitutional clause that limited voting to white men with property), Clinton would be president today.

Of those 65,853,516 voters, the majority were women—black, white, Hispanic, Native American, Asian, young, old, and blue-, pink-, and white-collar. Further, Clinton won young women (ages 18 to 29) handily and in significantly greater measure than men in the same age range. As I mentioned earlier, women will be the majority of presidential-election voters for decades to come if the pattern of the last four decades holds, so these young women and those coming up right behind them can coalesce with women of older generations to elect our first woman president.

Together in 2016, all of these women created a 24 percent gender gap—that is, the difference between men's and women's choice of candidate. The significant size of this gender gap—the largest one on record since exit polls started measuring it fifty years ago—shows how unified women of every kind were in voting for a woman candidate—significantly, one whose policies advanced equality and opportunity for every woman. As you know, their votes weren't in all the right places, but the pro-woman choice these women made convincingly demonstrates how much opportunity there is to mobilize other women, especially non-college-educated white women, to also vote in their self-interest and elect Madam President. Our task now is to organize together and build on the foundation we created in 2016 to unite as many of us—and as many types of us—as possible.

To do so, it's important to understand the nature of the opposition to electing Madam President. For instance, the size of the 2016 gender gap in the presidential race suggests that some men opposed a woman candidate simply because she was a woman. According to a survey conducted in June 2016 by the University of Michigan, "hostile attitudes toward women correlated with support for Trump": not particular women or a specific kind of woman but women in general. These attitudes reflect Clinton's comment during a 2017 interview with CNN's Fareed Zakaria that "sexism and misogyny are endemic in our society." As one *Newsweek* headline summarized, "The presidential election was a referendum on gender and women lost."

How else can we explain the fact that Clinton's extensive experience—both in government and in other kinds of public service—didn't matter? That Trump's steady stream of misogynistic language ("grab 'em by the pussy")—not to mention his seemingly total lack of commitment to deliberative governance and frightening ignorance about so much public policy—could not deter 62,984,825 people (46.4 percent of all voters) from voting for him?

Attorney General Lisa Madigan put it this way: "For women running for office, the issue has always been experience. With Hillary Clinton, we had the most qualified candidate, and suddenly, experience didn't matter."

Someday, A ♀ Will Be President

Clinton herself did not mince words in her own analysis in her book *What Happened*: "This has to be said: sexism and misogyny played a role in the 2016 presidential election. Exhibit A is that the flagrantly sexist candidate won. . . . Sexism exerts its pull on our politics and our society every day, in ways both subtle and crystal clear."

In too many men's eyes, there is no *right* way to be a woman when it comes to having political power. As Susan Bordo, author of *The Destruction of Hillary Clinton*, wrote in *Politico*:

> History suggests that the biggest obstacle to a woman aspiring to the highest office anywhere is simply that she is not a man. In every era, in every culture, as French philosopher Simone de Beauvoir pointed out, a man is the norm, and women are defined in terms of their difference from that norm. This is particularly true when it comes to our visual images and expectations for the head of state.

The very idea of a woman president—a woman possessing power over others that no other person would hold concurrently, being the most important decision maker in the world, and symbolizing the essence of the United States of America—was questioned in the 2016 presidential election. Turns out, most white men weren't having it. Apparently, they wanted nothing to do with a woman POTUS, even when she was vastly more qualified for the job than her male opponent. And, as a result, every woman—no matter what kind of woman—lost.

Yet, there is good news, too.

Those of us who marched a couple of months after the 2016 election understood the significance of this truth. Our understanding only deepened over the course of 2017, as we evaluated Trump's presidency. According to data from Erica Chenoweth at the University of Denver and Jeremy Pressman at the University of Connecticut, there were more than 8,700 protests in the United States between January 21, 2017, and December 31, 2017. About 74 percent of those protests were against Trump and his policies or views, drawing an estimated 5.9 million to 9 million people. Millions of us have kept up the trend by protesting at the 2018 Women's March and ever since.

> An estimated 5.9 million to 9 million people attended Trump-related protests in 2017.

More women than men show up to the polls. In fact, according to CAWP, there have been more women than men voting in every presidential election since 1964. We just need to continue this trend while uniting all women to elect our first woman president.

We likely will have a diverse group of women candidates to choose from as we embark on this common cause. The millions of women marchers, the tens of thousands of women interested in running for office, and the hundreds who are running suggest that 2018 could, as the *New York Daily News* said, "easily eclipse 1992 as the 'Year of the Woman' in American government." These candidates are of every racial and ethnic background and from all kinds of families and neighborhoods. They hold all kinds of jobs. They are at least as qualified as their male opponents for holding public office, including the presidency.

Here are two such examples of women who recently won executive office. Vi Lyles and LaToya Cantrell, the newly elected African American mayors of Charlotte, North Carolina, and New Orleans, Louisiana, respectively, are individuals with a deep and long-standing commitment to government service and community activism. (It appears that in 2018, more black women are serving in public office and running for public office than ever before in our nation's history.) During her career of several decades in Charlotte's city government, Lyles rose from budget analyst to budget director and to assistant city manager. Cantrell rose to prominence by advocating to the Louisiana governor and New Orleans mayor and city council members on behalf of her neighborhood after Hurricane Katrina devastated New Orleans in 2005. When Lyles and Cantrell ran for executive office, both had significant experience with decision-making processes in the executive context, just like Hillary Clinton did.

A decade ago, Clinton was a strong candidate in the Democratic presidential primary, and less than ten years later, she took a big step forward and became the Democratic Party nominee. Back then, it was nearly impossible to imagine that there would be African American women serving as mayors of so many cities. Or that an out lesbian, Annise Parker, would serve—three terms, no less—as mayor of the nation's fourth-largest city. Or that an African American woman, Stacey Abrams, might be elected governor of a formerly Confederate state. Or that a transgender person, Danica Roem, would be elected to the legislature of the state that was once the capital of the Confederacy. Or that a Liberian refugee, Wilmot Collins, would be elected mayor of Helena, Montana, a city where less than 1 percent of the population is black. But all this has happened. Clearly, over the course of this last decade, American voters have undergone a significant change in attitudes about women and minorities holding political office and thus opened the door to the political C-suite to women of every kind. Why should the door to the presidency stay closed?

Because we all ought to know in our hearts and minds that there is no wrong way to be a woman, what does it matter if the next woman candidate for president isn't perfect? What man or woman is? What presidential candidate is? What president is, as we have learned so distressingly from Donald Trump? The fact that no woman candidate needs to be perfect—just like no male one does either—offers opportunity for *every woman.*

Finally, some candidates—and some voters—may not be comfortable naming themselves feminists, but no matter: odds are they want to preserve and advance women's opportunities.

In our numbers and our diversity lie our strength and security. To me, this truth argues ever more powerfully that every kind of woman, whether she calls herself a feminist or not, whether she's a Democrat or a Republican, should favor electing a woman president. Each of us has a responsibility to reach beyond our own circle to connect with women who are different from us, foster a sense of unity and sisterhood, and convince each other that Madam President will work in our best interest, no matter who we are or which one of us ends up sitting behind the Oval Office desk. We are all in this together.

YOUR ACTION PLAN: UNITE

❑ **Create occasions with women different from you that are purely joyful, with no political or issue agenda, to gather and celebrate women's diversity.** For instance, gather your activist friends to celebrate holidays or each other's birthdays to signal that your relationships with them are not only professional but also personal. Such occasions will reinforce both the unity required for effective action and the idea that women of every kind can work together.

❑ **Organize community projects that help women and girls—of every kind—solve the common problems they face together.** These projects don't need to be explicitly about women's and girls' issues (e.g., sexual assault), but they should address challenges that many women face in their everyday lives, such as street crime, lack of affordable housing, or too few neighborhood playgrounds for their children. The purposes of these projects are both to solve a community problem *and* to demonstrate how women can collaborate to better women's lives. You don't need to do this on your own—you can identify neighborhood organizations that share your concerns and volunteer or partner with them.

❏ **Initiate programs or projects in your workplace that put diverse women in positions of executive responsibility.** If you already have a supervisory role in your workplace, step up and identify ways to increase the number and diversity of its women executives. If you don't have a supervisory role, lobby those who do. And don't stop there—watch what happens, and make sure that the changes you recommend are made or, if not, that there was a valid reason for not promoting a woman.

❏ **Don't ever turn down a chance to speak to or meet young women and girls so that you can motivate them to become leaders and advocate for women.** State's Attorney Kim Foxx told me "there isn't a school function I'm invited to I don't go to." Don't pass up any of your own opportunities to connect with girls and women in your community. Think about volunteering to speak at career days, athletic events, or other occasions where you can inspire, lead, or mentor girls.

CHAPTER 14

THE FUTURE IS NASTY

ACTION: NAME THE ENEMY

Next, we name the enemy, and we explain why. Yes, the enemy—not the gentlemanly opponent of political myth, the person of goodwill whose views differ from ours but who is willing to meet and compromise. (How many of them have you ever met?) Yes, the enemy—the one walking toward us belligerently because he wants to win for his candidate, who is likely not Madam President.

TRAITOR. RACIST, UNQUALIFIED, MISOGYNIST PUSSY GRABBER. TWITLER. SCUMBAG. LOWLIFE. LIAR. FRAUD. WANNABE PIMP. These are just a few of the words marchers used to name our enemy, Donald Trump, revealing their deep objections to him. Another poster, NYET TRUMP ("No Trump" in Russian), summed up marchers' sentiments.

In my experience, winning social justice campaigns requires naming the enemy. In the case of an electoral campaign, this can be done by clearly characterizing the personal qualities of your opponent that make him unsuited for the office sought. In the case of an issue advocacy campaign that complements an electoral campaign, naming the enemy means naming the specific problems with the opponent's position on the issue. In either circumstance, naming the enemy convincingly enough to induce political change—so that the threat he poses is understood *as a systemic one*—requires characterizing that person in the context of broader societal values, norms, and policy ideas. Once you name the enemy, then you are ready to organize and run a campaign that defeats him.

Consider the example of the 2012 US Senate race in Missouri when incumbent Senator Claire McCaskill's opponent Rep. Todd Akin asserted there is such a thing as "legitimate rape." Hello, tenth-grade biology class! Hello, no evidence of any moral compass or of any commitment to the societal norm that rape is wrong. McCaskill named Akin and his belief the enemy. Akin lost. McCaskill won.

Unfortunately, women don't always win against ignorant or, apparently, women-hating men. Too often, these men are evaluated in political and cultural contexts that writer Jill Filipovic calls "misogynist norms." In 2016, too many women voters fell prey to accepting these norms, voting for a man who views women as "pussy." Too many voters didn't care that Trump habitually denigrated women, frequently calling them disgusting names. Remember "Crooked Hillary"? This was said by a man who reportedly stiffed his vendors on a regular basis. A man who allegedly engaged in fraudulent behavior. Remember Trump University? Trump had to settle for millions to make those charges go away.

How sad that an individual like Donald Trump could be elected after his personal behavior and comments placed him so outside the norm of our commonly shared values, such as honesty and respect for others. How sad that his aberrant behavior wasn't a sufficient reason to vote for his opponent. To me, this outcome proves the importance of naming the enemy, as pointedly as possible.

Perhaps the women who voted for Trump believed that, despite his language and behavior, he would treat them respectfully and fairly. Perhaps they thought he was just kidding around, as some have repeatedly insisted even after multiple reports of his sexual impropriety and harassment.

Tragically, these women voters have now been proven wrong. Personal beliefs on matters of gender that Trump expressed on the campaign trail have

Traitor
Racist
Unqualified
Misogynist
Pussy Grabber

influenced policy decisions that are detrimental to millions of women, including those who voted for him. A telling example is his ongoing effort to weaken, if not destroy, Planned Parenthood through federal funding restrictions.

Trump's demonstrated lack of respect for women helps undermine the notion that men are *ever* just kidding around when they engage in sexual harassment (or worse). At this point, that idea has become so hard to justify that some Christians who voted for Trump are relying on their beliefs in God's forgiveness to come to grips with Trump's alleged bad behavior. According to Tony Perkins, president of the Family Research Council, a conservative Christian nonprofit group, "Among evangelicals, there's an understanding that we are all fallen, and the idea of forgiveness is very prominent." The best rationale that Rev. Franklin Graham could come up with was "I appreciate the fact that the president does have a concern for Christian values." Happily, these justifications may no longer suffice for some evangelical Christian women who voted for Trump. According to a 2018 survey by Pew, a statistically significant number of white evangelical women are "tiptoeing away" from their support of him.

What are we to make of the rhetorical lengths to which men will go to try to convince women they have their interests at heart when their actions demonstrate otherwise? For instance, today's Republican men in office—led by President Trump—have urged the US Supreme Court to weaken public sector unions (whose members include millions of women), jeopardized access to health care for children and low-income families, and proposed draconian cutbacks to the Supplemental Nutrition Assistance Program, "food stamps." The women officials who partner with these men are not blameless, but the men are conducting the train.

What are we to make of the fact that systemic misogynistic norms like those embedded in these actions must be overcome to elect our first woman president? Our first lesson is to be woke and willing to name the enemy—always. We must take candidates at their word and encourage others to do the same. If more women had taken Trump at his word—in, say, those big states like Michigan, Ohio, Wisconsin, Florida, and Pennsylvania—he might have lost.

Second, we must recognize that in the 2016 presidential campaign, no matter what most white men heard or read or viewed about Trump's misogynistic behavior, it didn't matter; most of them voted for Trump. No more acceding to the notion that boys will be boys. No more assuming that when it comes to matters of women's fair treatment, men will do the right thing. We must name men the enemy when their actions make it clear they are. We cannot depend on them. We must depend on ourselves. "Denying women's suffrage was not accidental," State's Attorney Kim Foxx told me. "We have to repair what that exclusion has done. It caused great harm to this country." I love her idea for a solution: "That hurt widens the gaps the longer we carry this legacy of not electing a woman president."

Third, we always need to remember that naming the enemy is a complex process that begins with naming only. *Name-calling* won't suffice. *Naming*—going beyond pejorative words to identify and describe the specific reasons a candidate is unfit for the office he seeks—is a constant task.

When thinking about the importance of naming the enemy and explaining why you chose that naming, remember that American women have never been on equal political footing with American men. For instance, until women won federal suffrage in 1920, men with political power continually asserted that women weren't deserving of the foundational responsibility of a democracy—the right to vote for those who govern them. But, almost 175 years ago, in Seneca Falls, New York, the suffragists who wrote and signed the Declaration of Sentiments named American men's "absolute tyranny" over American women as their enemy and outlined in their evidence women's lack of the vote. In part, their declaration reads:

To prove this, let facts be submitted to a candid world.

He has never permitted her to exercise her inalienable right to the elective franchise.

He has compelled her to submit to laws, in the formation of which she had no voice. . . .

Having deprived her of this first right of a citizen, the elective franchise, thereby leaving her without representation in the halls of legislation, he has oppressed her on all sides.

He has made her, if married, in the eye of the law, civilly dead.

He has taken from her all right in property, even to the wages she earns.

What other word than *tyranny* could be used to characterize men's denying the constitutional right to women's universal suffrage until the twentieth century? Men feared giving up their absolute power. Had women not been feared as enemies who, if granted voting rights might become public officials with power over men, would women have been prevented from voting? Likely not. No wonder electing a woman president has been so difficult!

Tellingly, men opposed to women's suffrage didn't name women as the enemy. Instead, they obfuscated and argued that women didn't belong in the public sphere or need the vote. Here is a revealing passage describing the depth of opposition to women's suffrage, over sixty years after the Declaration of Sentiments made a compelling case for it. In 1911, J. B. Sanford, the chairman of the Democratic Caucus of the California State Senate, said, "Politics is no place for a [woman;] consequently the privilege [of suffrage] should not be granted to her." Worse yet, assuming every woman is a mother, Sanford continued:

The mother's influence is needed in the home. She can do little good by gadding the streets and neglecting her children. . . . The mothers of this country can shape the destinies of the nation by keeping in their places and attending to those duties that God Almighty intended for them. The kindly, gentle influence of the mother in the home and the dignified influence of the teacher in the school will far outweigh all the influence of all the mannish female politicians on earth. . . .

The men are able to run the government and take care of the women. . . . By keeping woman in her exalted position man can be induced to do more for her than he could by having her mix up in affairs that will cause him to lose respect and regard for her. Woman does not have to vote to secure her rights.

At the outset of this chapter, I made the point that, when naming the enemy, it is important that the threat the enemy poses is clearly understood *as a systemic one* perpetrated by government policy. Thomas Jefferson, the writer of the Declaration of Independence, and Elizabeth Cady Stanton, the writer of the Declaration of Sentiments, both named systemic government oppression as their enemy. Both Jefferson and Stanton named and condemned a political infrastructure of beliefs, actions, and laws resulting in inequitable treatment. To elect the first American woman president, we have to be willing to do the same.

With that in mind, let's name two enemies ahead of our next campaign to elect Madam President: the first is the sex discrimination rampant in American society. The second is any man who endorses and perpetuates this discrimination. We will name these men as enemies until they demonstrate clear support for a pro-woman agenda. Our message will be, we're happy to have you along for the ride, but if you aren't with us, you will be named as the enemy. The future will be nasty if need be.

As we move forward, remember that no woman is an enemy, even if she does not share all of your political beliefs. She may be misinformed or misguided, but she is not the enemy. We are sisters, sharing a common biological and cultural framework because we are women. We are women dedicated to educating each other about what is best for all of us, explaining why every modern woman's best interests are served by electing a woman president, just as every woman's best interests in 1920 were served by securing the right to vote.

YOUR ACTION PLAN: NAME THE ENEMY

❑ **Name the enemy based on his wrongheaded personal traits, beliefs, or policy positions that generate inequality between American men and women in the political sphere.** While it's important to make it clear that American gender discrimination is systemic, the most effective way to name the enemy is to personalize the naming. Consequently, you will need to identify the specific aspects of Madam President's opponent that make him unqualified or unfit to govern women because his policies will perpetuate this systemic discrimination. This inventory must be created on a case-by-case basis because there are nuances to candidate policy positions that need to be considered and evaluated.

❑ **Identify the opposition's message, and state a positive counter-message that your Madam President candidate embodies.** This message should be one that resonates among women who have not yet been convinced that personal expressions of anti-women attitudes yield bad public policy. In this context, think about examples of anti-women policies you have endured. Then extrapolate from those the systemic challenge that anti-women policies reflect. For example, think about unequal pay or other workplace conditions that negatively affect women. Then state your counter-message, such as, "Equal pay for equal work." Keep saying it.

❑ **Lead political campaigns, whether as a volunteer or as a staffer.** While the number of women who lead political campaigns is increasing, there is still a long way to go to reach parity. Without parity, we don't hear women's voices in sufficient numbers on the issues that these campaigns address.

The reasons to lead a campaign are manifold. These leaders frame and deliver the candidate's core messages and policy positions.

Campaign leaders are the face of the candidate. Think about the potential damage done when potential voters see young men representing women candidates. What's up with that? Wouldn't a woman's face and a woman's voice describing Madam President's commitments to women resonate so much more? Yes, it would, for the same reasons that product marketers select spokespeople who share characteristics with prospective product purchasers. Identifying with customers leads to sales; identifying with constituents leads to votes.

Campaign leaders also answer the tough questions, whether related to policy or to the candidate's personal characteristics or history. Campaign leaders refute characterizations to set the record straight. They also can connect what may appear to be narrow policy ideas to broader systemic problems, and in that process, call out discrimination against their candidate (consider how Hillary Clinton was scrutinized during the 2016 presidential election campaign, compared with how Donald Trump was).

There are both paid leaders and volunteer leaders on a campaign. For instance, the campaign manager is likely paid, but the chairperson of the finance committee might not be. As someone committed to defeating the enemy, you have options. If you think you're suited for political leadership of any sort—especially if you want to run for office someday—consider stepping up to lead a campaign. The lessons you learn will hold you in good stead.

CHAPTER 15

IT IS TIME TO USE OUR OUTSIDE VOICES

ACTION: SPEAK

The duty to speak is a matter of principle, not a ministerial or tactical assignment. And because it is a matter of principle, it is a perpetual responsibility. Marchers took this duty seriously by coming together and making their voices heard loud and clear. One sign read IT'S TIME TO USE OUR OUTSIDE VOICES, and the marchers did, calling on sister marchers and their allies to speak up and advocate for the political changes that matter most to women—including electing our first woman president.

The Women's Marches in 2017 and 2018 confirmed the power of women's collective outside voice, one that is assertive, confident, unified, and committed to political action that benefits women. The marchers left no doubt about their willingness to shout to the rooftops together a pledge to secure justice for every woman. Their posters underscored this commitment. For instance, marchers repeatedly proclaimed I WILL NOT GO QUIETLY BACK TO THE 1950S, a time when, like children, too often women were seen but not heard; when women's political equality was but a dream; and when most women feared speaking publicly about policy and political matters, much less in an outside voice.

But while the collective speaks with its outside voice, each of us still has the power and the duty to speak individually. But how? How does each

woman—and especially when no other woman may be around to join her—keep speaking with her outside voice? Even when people are listening and following our lead, how do we speak convincingly? How do we take responsibility for continually speaking in order to make sure the changes we advocate actually occur?

Ai-jen Poo, director of the National Domestic Workers Alliance and codirector of Caring Across Generations, wrote in an essay about the 2017 Women's March that continuing the momentum from the March is our responsibility to take with us every day, everywhere. She wrote that "a woman's work is never done when our democracy is at stake." She suggested that every space where women gather—every dinner table, break room, locker room, meeting room, park bench, wherever—creates a context in which to work for democracy. One of my heroines, Dolores Huerta, an organizer of American farmworkers and a civil rights activist, stated this point succinctly (years earlier): "Every moment is an organizing opportunity, every person a potential activist, every minute a chance to change the world."

Some of us are more comfortable than others when it comes to speaking up, but each one of us has the power to do it. If you ever need an extra push, remember that your outside voice can feel very personal to others and, therefore, be highly effective. When you are willing to speak assertively to others—in any context in which you find yourself—regarding a matter of social justice or political equality that you are passionate about, people sit up and take notice. Speaking with your outside voice is an act that takes courage, and people respect that.

Now, there could be some fallout. You might be viewed as out of line. You might be criticized for what you say just for saying it. You might be viewed as a trouble maker, especially if the people in your life aren't used to hearing you speaking politically or if political organizing isn't your profession. Conversely, if political organizing *is* your profession, people may brush you off—"Oh, that's just something she gets paid to do. Just like I get paid to talk about the product I'm selling." Don't let them do that.

Political speech is not like product marketing speech, even when said by those who are paid to do it. Political speech addresses the core of our values and beliefs. Pitched in an outside voice to attract, influence, and persuade an audience, it speaks to cultural norms and societal behavior, advocating changes in community beliefs, individual actions, and laws. That is a big deal. Advocating a certain brand of makeup, or fried chicken, or cat food, or even purchasing organic vegetables is useful, but it *isn't* a big deal. Promoting consumer products doesn't lead to systemic change, unlike, say, a political rally and follow-up advocacy campaign do because rallies and campaigns enable us to use our outside voices joining others doing the same. Sadly, political speech can be hateful, but yours won't be. Your political speech in your outside voice will advance the notion of systemic change that benefits women, making the world a better place.

American heroines have recognized the need for systemic change benefiting women and their responsibility to use their outside voice to speak frankly to the men in power who could make those changes. In one early example of this, Abigail Adams sent a letter to her husband, John Adams, and his fellow members of the Continental Congress in March 1776, urging them to consider women's rights as they founded the new nation:

> By the way, in the new code of laws which I suppose it will be necessary for you to make, I desire you would remember the ladies and be more generous and favorable to them than your ancestors. Do not put such unlimited power into the hands of the husbands. Remember, all men would be tyrants if they could. If particular care and attention is not paid to the ladies, we are determined to foment a rebellion, and will not hold ourselves bound by any laws in which we have no voice or representation.

We don't know what actions John Adams took as a result of reading Abigail Adams's letter, but we do know that her ideas have resonated through the ages, inspiring other women to speak in their outside voice. That's the whole idea.

More recently, another revolutionary—singer, actress, and activist Janelle Monáe—spoke in *her* outside voice. At the 2018 Grammy Awards, speaking about the recent tsunami of sexual harassment accusations against male executives in the entertainment industry that sparked the #TimesUp and #MeToo movements, Monáe declared:

> We come in peace, but we mean business. And to those who would dare try and silence us, we offer you two words: time's up. We say, time's up for pay inequality, time's up for discrimination, time's up for harassment of any kind, and time's up for the abuse of power. . . . And just as we have the power to shape culture, we also have the power to undo the culture that does not serve us well.

Two hundred and forty-two years separate these two statements from two women of one mind. However, they spoke in the same outside voice: singularly and frankly, as each occasion demanded. This is exactly what you need to do to help elect our first woman president—speak to every woman, using every platform you have. Monáe stated our assignment plainly: "we mean business," and that business begins with each woman becoming part of the "we" by speaking out.

I argue in this book that electing the first woman president is our American revolution. It seems to me that Abigail Adams, too, dreamed of this possibility: "We are determined to foment a rebellion, and will not hold ourselves bound by any laws in which we have no voice or representation." That rebellion of hers—and ours—begins with speaking in our outside voices.

YOUR ACTION PLAN: SPEAK

❏ **Tell your own story, publicly.** Our American revolution is about telling women's stories, and that includes you and your story. Speak up by sharing your story with other women, using your own words and your outside voice. You may have noticed that those in the public eye like to tell their stories in their own words so that they are viewed in the most favorable light. This is the same reason you hear celebrities, business leaders, and politicians tell their stories frequently. That way, they "control the narrative," as political consultants put it. Of course, in an era of media saturation and a 24/7 news cycle, nothing less would work anyway. So always remember: people will find your story and draw their own conclusions. Best that you tell it first in that outside voice of yours.

An additional benefit of this practice is that, as you shape and tell your story, you can shape the rationale for Madam President, too. Your story can also underscore the validity, larger purposes, and benefits of women as public leaders, in whatever capacity they serve.

Clerk Anna Valencia advised that when you speak, "be open and authentic about what has impelled you to speak and lead." Your authenticity will also create empathy, emotionally connecting you to others who have similar concerns and interests, such as in electing our first woman president. This practice will encourage your listeners to do the same, thereby making the case for a Madam President who is an open and authentic woman leader.

❏ **Speak in order to advance other women's political speech that promotes women's equality.** Doing so will help advance women's equality and foster a climate conducive to electing Madam President. Consequently, each time you speak, make the most inclusive remarks you can. Your speech is always for every woman, intended to motivate every woman to join you in electing Madam President. When you do this, do as Clerk Valencia advised and "keep your word."

❑ **Decide when, how, and where to speak out, using others' words to elevate your own.** When you select and apply evaluative criteria before you speak out, you will have a bigger impact. Assessing the context, the likely audience, and how the speaking opportunity fits into the larger mission to elect Madam President will enable you to write and speak convincingly.

Putting your words into the context of others' speech will also enhance your impact. You can quote, paraphrase, or refer to lines of poetry or passages of a novel to elevate your speech and make it part of a bigger cause. That's what great speeches accomplish—tailored to their time, place, and listeners, they motivate, inspire, and impel action. That's the only kind of speech you ever want to give.

❑ **Defend the speech of your sisters when they misstep.** For many years, I had a client who was a very devout Catholic. As we worked together on programs to improve health care services for women and enlisted the support of important politicians and businesspeople in our cause, she was wont to say: "Remember, Rebecca, we are all equals in the eyes of God." I didn't need to be religious to understand her message: we are all equals and, as a result, we are all equally deserving of help when we falter.

❑ **During our campaign to elect Madam President, she will falter,** *and so will we.* Forgive her as you would forgive any other sister. I am not referring to speaking dishonestly but to speaking too casually or too lightly. We must protect her as she rises and one another, too, as we rise in our sisterhood of mutual care.

CHAPTER 16

I AM NOT FREE WHILE ANY WOMAN IS UNFREE

ACTION: CONNECT

After uniting in our belief that there is no wrong way to be a woman, there is great joy in connecting with people from different backgrounds. This sentiment was expressed in many Women's March posters. One sign read FIGHT FOR WHAT'S RIGHT with a universal women's symbol drawn next to the words. Another proclaimed MÁS FUERTES JUNTOS. STRONGER TOGETHER. A third simply said ALLY.

I have already discussed the importance of women building bridges to connect in coalitions across ethnic and racial boundaries, as well as across class lines. I know this is often easier said than done. In our march together to carry a woman into the Oval Office, there will be times when we must work hard to understand and overcome deep differences—political, spiritual, and cultural—in order to achieve a better state of the union for all women. But that purpose is well worth achieving.

It was beautifully implicit in one marcher's poster. It read I AM NOT FREE WHILE ANY WOMAN IS UNFREE. Her words still ring in my ears. How can we be content if our neighbor is hungry or homeless? How can we be content when, in some nearby neighborhood, women have children who do not have good schools or safe playgrounds, or who aren't safe walking down the street or knocking on a neighbor's door? How can we be content when women we know are paid less than their male coworkers or subordinates, or are forced to work in unsafe environments? I know you understand me: we ought not to be content even if we think we can be. We are not free until all other women are, too. We are not free until we can connect with other women to solve problems and create solutions, such as electing our first woman president.

After the American Revolution, the writers of the Constitution embarked on a political campaign to convince the states to ratify it. Part of their strategy was to publish a series of letters, now called *The Federalist Papers*, whose initial purpose was to convince New York to ratify. (Some of the letters were subsequently published in other states.)

In all, there were eighty-five essays. One of the most lasting in relation to our current form of federal governance is *Federalist,* no. 10. It was written by James Madison (who later became the fourth US president), in part to make the argument that the larger the body of government and the more diverse the interests of its representatives, the less likely any one interest group would dominate federal policy making.

Madison's argument centered on the idea of safety in numbers because he was concerned about potential disunity due to interest groups devolving into what he termed "factions." But he also recognized—and therein lies the genius of *Federalist,* no. 10—that the greater the number of people with different ideas and interests who could meet and legislate together, the more impetus there would be to create a common good.

This idea might be hard to swallow in today's fractious political climate. However, I think the United States may not be any more fractious today than it was then. At the time that *The Federalist Papers* were written, many weren't convinced there was *any* need for a government beyond a loose confederation of sovereign states.

Madison's premise is the cornerstone of the coalition building required to elect our first woman president: mobilizing women with differing interests and ideas to achieve positive outcomes for all. In Madison's case, the common interest was building a strong federal government among states with little inclination to work together. In our case, it is building a strong federal government led by a woman who will benefit factions of women also in states too often not inclined to work together.

One marcher's poster described this process as CONNECT. PROTECT. ACTIVATE. We already know that we can: a substantial array of factions of women already voted for a woman presidential candidate—just not quite enough in a few key states.

Finding Gender in Election 2016 is the final report of Presidential Gender Watch 2016, a project created to "track, analyze, and illuminate gender dynamics in the 2016 presidential election." The project's creators, the Barbara Lee Family Foundation and CAWP, were at pains to be both objective and nonpartisan in their report. That's their job. However, the conclusion got to the bald

truth about the 2016 presidential campaign: "It [the report] reveals evidence of the maintenance of masculine dominance in presidential politics, as well as signs of institutional change that may expand our ideas of what and whom is deemed presidential." One of these signs of institutional change is the fact that a woman can now be a credible major-party candidate for the presidency. But that fact didn't have sufficient power to overcome the ongoing gender bias regarding who should be president. In the minds of many, that role still belongs to men.

This manifesto is all about changing men's *and* women's minds on this topic. But we can't accomplish that unless we connect with one another. To do so, we need to build on the knowledge of what united us in 2016 while avoiding what separated us. In order to do this and win, we must remember to fight for what connects us because no woman is free while any woman is unfree.

YOUR ACTION PLAN: CONNECT

❑ **Identify and connect with diverse groups of people.** If you only connect with people like you, you won't deliver positive results for Madam President. The numbers just won't add up to a victory. If you haven't met and understood those who are different from you, how can you partner effectively going forward?

Your connecting with diverse groups of people isn't only about winning a political race. It's about winning a leadership role in the public space for you, too. When you connect across differences, you can learn what matters to all the members of your community and be better positioned to help them accomplish their shared goals.

❑ **Build camaraderie among people from different personal backgrounds and life and work experiences.** I have already recommended using celebratory occasions as a strategy for making the case and generating the sentiment that every woman of every kind is welcome on this mission of ours. Here, I emphasize following up on those celebratory occasions by engaging in other activities with those people. Bonding with them at a fund-raising or protest event will not only increase the likelihood of that event's success because it has diverse communities' support but also will make our larger point: every woman can be an integral part of electing our first woman president, and, therefore, every woman can benefit once she is in office.

❑ **Understand that political connection need not include sharing your personal life in order for the political effort to be meaningful and effective.** Recently, a younger colleague starting out in her public leadership career asked me whether she had to tell a family story about sexual violence to legitimize her strong advocacy for punishment of rapists and abusers. I said no, explaining that it was sufficient for her to say she felt strongly and substantiate her strong feelings with a powerful policy case because her experience was clearly too painful to have to recount. Of course, she would have to remain cognizant of what could be found in public records, but she had no duty to be vulnerable. Madam President will need our support in similar circumstances. Human frailties go with being human. So as we campaign for her, we will protect her privacy, the same way we protect our own.

❑ **Assert the joy that is connection, especially when fights are lost, as they sometimes will be.** I hope this statement speaks for itself. In the campaign to do the right thing—that is, to elect our first woman president—there is joy to be found in the doing *and* in the knowing that you are doing your best. Assert that joy whenever necessary.

CHAPTER 17

RESPECT EXISTENCE OR EXPECT RESISTANCE

ACTION: RESIST

A male president has been the norm for the entire history of our nation. For over half that time, I argue, women's existence wasn't respected because women couldn't vote. In the face of these truths, what better idea than RESPECT EXISTENCE OR EXPECT RESISTANCE describes our response? What better word than *resist* characterizes the political action required to rid ourselves of this norm and elect our first woman president?

When the *New York Times* asked several activists what *resist* means to them in the current era, here is what political and arts consultant Aisha Dew said:

> "Resist" means to stand for the people who already make America great. The United States is diverse because we are a country of immigrants who came to America for freedom and a better way of life. Although I am the descendant of slaves, I recognize that there are many who came here to escape starvation, death, persecution and war. And as a descendant of slaves, I know that America has been challenged throughout history to deliver on its promise of freedom for all, but has also been slowly moving toward justice for all.

Dew claimed, and I agree, that the duty to resist oppression or discrimination is an essential component of being an American. One marcher made this duty clear by demanding, TRUMP—KEEP YOUR HANDS OFF MY BODY, MY RIGHTS, MY COUNTRY. Another marcher replaced an image of Rosie the Riveter on her poster with one of Michelle Obama, arm raised, fist clenched, and declared TIME TO GET TO WORK. 2020, suggesting there is no time to waste not resisting.

Resistance is necessary, even, as many marchers declared, by those who seem to have it all. Even they are constrained by systemic discriminatory forces. There was a MELANIA: YES, YOU CAN poster, pointing out that any woman, anywhere, can resist discrimination and hatred. At first, I thought the point about Melania Trump was trivial. But then I changed my mind—every woman has a responsibility to use her voice to resist. Melania Trump and others of her economic class also have money to donate to women's causes, as well as circles of wealthy friends and colleagues they can encourage to donate and resist. The duty to resist falls on every woman, no matter her position in the world. For instance, just as Melania Trump advocates children's health—at the same time as her husband is proposing to cut back funding for the federal Children's Health Insurance Program—she could, for instance, advocate women's health.

Of course, our resistance must insist on respect for our existence, as many of the marchers pointedly proclaimed Donald Trump does not. As I mentioned earlier, he was named "Twitler," "racist," and "misogynist." In the mind of that marcher, "Twitler" must be resisted *now*. Trump should expect resistance *now*.

While Trump's actions are frightening and racist, at least at the moment the comparison between "Twitler" and Hitler is inaccurate. Those who resisted Hitler's Germany risked death and millions were murdered. *The Zookeeper's Wife: A War Story*, a book by Diane Ackerman that was adapted into a film in 2017, is the story of a woman who hid and cared for Jews in Warsaw during Germany's occupation of Poland in World War II. I recently read a similarly courageous story, *The Nazi Officer's Wife: How One Jewish Woman Survived the Holocaust* by Edith Hahn Beer with Susan Dworkin. Beer, a Jewish

woman, had gone underground and reemerged as a Christian woman in order to survive in Nazi Germany. Jews have not gone underground or had to hide in Twitler's United States.

I understand how difficult and personally dangerous resistance is for some women. In *State Crime, Women and Gender,* author Victoria E. Collins wrote about the Egyptians who protested human rights abuses in Tahrir Square in Cairo in 2011: "Sexual violence against women occurred during many of the protests in Egypt. . . . sexual assault was prevalent. . . . What becomes apparent is that women resisters of state-perpetrated violence can be differentiated from their male counterparts as they are not only mobilizing for change and engaging in the same behaviors as men, but they face secondary threats to their security based solely on their sex and gender."

In the face of mortal danger or sexual assault, your duty is to resist only to the extent that you can. Remember this: no one can say that what you've done is not enough if you've done everything you can without putting your own life in peril. It is the act of resistance itself that matters most. Your duty is to act. Your duty is to speak in that outside voice of yours. Your duty is to declare an agenda that benefits women, whether in a letter you write, a petition you sign, or a march you join. Your duty is to resist if countered. I promise you will find yourself in good company. Indeed, our world is full of examples of women resisting.

Oftentimes, history's heroines are found in the most unlikely of places and circumstances, undertaking the most heroic of acts, thereby underscoring the power of women's resistance. Think about Malala Yousafzai in rural Pakistan, who resisted the Taliban and insisted that women

> No one can say that what you've done is not enough if you've done everything you can without putting your own life in peril.

and children in Pakistan be educated. Other young women have resisted as she did, exhibiting great courage in seemingly modest but universally emblematic acts. Think about the Freedom Riders of the Civil Rights Movement, who resisted by riding buses throughout the South to challenge segregation and put pressure on the federal government to enforce Supreme Court decisions that ruled against segregation on interstate buses. Or think about the civil rights activists who created the Mississippi Freedom Schools to teach African American history in order to encourage their dispossessed African American students to become political advocates for their rights.

Here is the inspirational story of another young woman, Mavis Staples—a world-renowned blues and gospel singer and civil rights activist. From a young age, Staples was the lead singer of her family's musical group, the Staple Singers, who sang to mobilize resisters at Civil Rights Movement meetings, church services, political rallies, and other occasions where resistance to racism was on the agenda.

I was honored to work with Staples as part of a radio advertising campaign to encourage African American participation in the US Census. She had volunteered to record the radio spot; all she had asked for was a car to get her to the recording studio that a friend of mine had donated for the session. Another friend, a childhood friend of Staples, had introduced us so that I could ask her to participate in the campaign—though approximately twenty-five years earlier, she and I had met when my husband and I attended a Staple Singers performance at the Burning Spear, a greatly missed Chicago blues club. There were no empty seats when we arrived, so Roebuck "Pops" Staples, Staples's father and the founder of the Staple Singers, invited us to sit at the family table!

In 1965, the Staple Singers released an album titled *Freedom Highway*, which featured a song by the same name that Pops had written shortly after the march from Selma to Montgomery, Alabama. Over half a century later, in 2017, Mavis was back on the freedom highway:

It's like we have to start all over again. It's worse than it was in the '60s because we have this man—I don't like to speak his name—bringing out the worst in us. . . . The people in Puerto Rico being treated like they aren't worth his time, the racist (Charlottesville, Va., white nationalist) march, him calling people names. 'Crooked Hillary'? Who says that sort of thing except a bully? This man is not a president. I won't call him a thug, but he acts like one.

It's time for all of us to get back on the freedom highway, resisting as we march.

YOUR ACTION PLAN: RESIST

❏ **Assess your circumstances and opportunities to determine the right resistance action(s) for you.** Not all acts of resistance are equal, but each has value when it connects to your beliefs and is organized to make an impact. For example, if you are not a marcher but you are a writer, resist by writing about your ideas or about women who lead. If you are not a singer, you can still organize a concert. If you have never been a political activist before but you now understand why Madam President is such a good idea, share your understanding with others. Resist in every way you can and as hard and as often as you can.

❏ **Develop a public presence as a resister, and encourage others to do the same.** You can promote yourself on print and social media platforms, in organizational settings, and in the workplace (as appropriate). In each context, highlight your acts of resistance to motivate others to join you.

❏ **Create networks among those who agree with your message and your acts of resistance.** Creating this network is like creating any other kind of network: you will ask others to join you in a common endeavor. Your goal will be to recruit as many others as you can to join you in your acts of resistance and, in return, you will join in theirs. Just imagine what your group can accomplish together!

If you need inspiration for this activity, think about how the Women's March was organized, and why it has had such a big impact. One woman after another recruited her friends and family members to resist with her. For your acts of resistance, you will do the same.

❑ **Be an ally of other women who are resisting.** Because there is both safety and power in numbers, become an ally and defend other women who choose to resist. These are the women in the network you have created, as well as women you don't know but whose resistance you believe in. It takes courage to do resistance work, so every woman deserves support for choosing it.

You also will ally with others to resist on a larger scale. For example, if your first experience with resistance was participating in the Women's March and now you're feeling committed, think about creating alliances for larger, ongoing campaigns, such as electing our first woman president!

Also, think long-term about *leading* issue campaigns that resist government inaction or discrimination. Your goal will be to build an allied force to be reckoned with.

❑ **Promote messages about collective acts of resistance that reject the norm of the American presidency (male presidents) to advance your collective's desire to elect Madam President.** These messages are the public education or media campaigns you create as part of your resistance. Follow the marchers' example, and be frank when engaging each resister to voice these messages.

CHAPTER 18   NOT AFRAID

ACTION: FIGHT

I know committed feminists who like neither the word *fight* nor the act of fighting. Even if they are not afraid, as a rule, they don't want to fight. They think fighting isn't for them because they view it as crass. Or they think they can win without fighting. Or they are willing to argue but only politely. Or *sometimes*, they will rally and march, but that's about it.

But polite arguments, rallying, and marching aren't sufficient to elect Madam President. If we once thought they were, the 2016 presidential campaign disabused us of that notion. Dozens of thoughtful speeches and exhaustive policy papers didn't make a difference either, and famous actresses taking up the cause didn't matter (enough). Once the opponent cries, "Lock her up!" with impunity, it is time to *fight*.

Fighting begins with developing a certain frame of mind. It means being willing to dig in relentlessly and match the opponent blow for blow. I've described in earlier chapters some of the actions you can take after you've developed this frame of mind, but first, think about how you will get to the place where you are eager to fight.

As I photographed her at the Women's March, a hip, fortyish African American woman wearing a leather jacket chose to hold high a sign that read

NOT AFRAID. Of the several hundred posters I photographed, only one other, carried by a young white woman, was as straightforward in its construction and lettering as hers. In black Magic Marker letters on brown cardboard, that young woman's sign simply said SOMEDAY, A WOMAN WILL BE PRESIDENT. The messages on these two posters were no less powerful than those on the multicolored, glittered, or elaborately collaged ones. They, too, got to the heart of the matter.

Consider the meaning of "not afraid" in the larger context of centuries of systemic discrimination against African Americans and the courage those Women's March resisters and others have demonstrated, while living their lives as best they can. Here is one such example from my experience. When my husband and I moved to Chicago, part of his job for a local jazz and blues record label was booking the label's bands. In 1976, we traveled to Port Arthur, Texas, with one of these bands. We drove through southern Illinois, Mississippi, and Arkansas, as well as down the length of Texas to get there. The African American members of the band—all first- or second-generation migrants to Chicago from Mississippi—refused to stop, except for gas. They insisted our meals be only snacks bought at these gas stations: not afraid to live your life does not mean acting imprudently. No sense in taking any chances, they thought, with two young white people in the van.

Over forty years later, I remember that trip vividly. Growing up in New York and attending college in Minnesota, I certainly had never had an experience like that before. In the mid-1970s, those musicians were not afraid to travel with whites through the South—there we were, just a dozen years after the Civil Rights Act was passed, traveling together—less than ten years after I had seen segregated water fountains on my family trip south. I share this story to make the point that as you decide to fight, including to argue and march, you will have to decide for yourself the limits of your battles. Like resisting, fighting ought to be everything you think you can do without being foolhardy.

The woman carrying the NOT AFRAID sign was one or two generations younger than those musicians. Perhaps she had heard family stories about the bad old days, which aren't all that old. According to the Equal Justice Initiative report *Lynching in America: Confronting the Legacy of Racial Terror*, there were close to 4,100 lynchings of African Americans in the southern United States between 1877 and 1950, shaping "the contemporary geographic, political, social, and economic conditions of African Americans . . . [including present-day] police abuse of people of color." Maybe as that marcher carried her sign, she thought about that present-day police abuse or the racist behavior Donald Trump condones. Her response: "Not afraid." Not afraid to publicly declare what she believed to be right—opposition to Donald Trump and his hateful and fearful agenda.

We need to be not afraid, too. We need to be willing to FIGHT LIKE A GIRL, as one young marcher's sign stated. She even drew smiley faces and heart-shaped images in crayon on her poster to underscore her point. How about taking inspiration from the country song "Fight Like a Girl" by the group Bomshel, in which they sing:

> So hold your head high
> Don't ever let them define
> The light in your eyes
> Love yourself, give 'em hell
> You can take on this world
> You just stand and be strong
> And then fight like a girl.

In our fight to elect our first woman president, let's heed the words of this poster and song: fight like girls, unafraid to express our self-love and our self-interest in electing a woman president who has our concerns first in her presidential heart. And who is a fighter, too.

The women who have run for president have all been fighters. I've already written here about Hillary Clinton and Shirley Chisholm, but before both of them, in the 1960s, there was Margaret Chase Smith, a Republican US senator from Maine. Talk about someone who was not afraid to fight!

Smith was born in Maine in 1897 and was well into adulthood before the Nineteenth Amendment was ratified in 1920. She served as a member of the US House of Representatives from 1940 to 1949 and then as a US senator from 1949 to 1973. She was the first woman elected to both House and Senate seats.

Smith was the oldest of six children in a blue-collar family. Growing up, she held jobs as a waitress, a store clerk, and a shoe factory worker. After high school, she was a teacher, a telephone operator, an office manager, and a staffer at a small newspaper. Her husband was elected to the House of Representatives, but, when he became ill, he convinced Smith to run. She won convincingly then and thereafter.

One of Smith's most significant legislative achievements was the Women's Armed Services Integration Act, which permitted women to serve as full members of the armed forces. The law was enacted in 1948 after World War

II, when about 350,000 women were members of the US armed forces but did not receive the same benefits as male members.

At a time when women had no legal right to apply for credit or keep a job if they were pregnant (those laws didn't change until the 1970s) and when the first woman had only been elected to the US House of Representatives 20 years earlier (over half of all the women elected to the House have been elected since 1992), Smith succeeded in the political arena. She was not afraid to fight. When a US Senate seat opened up in Maine and Smith sought her party's endorsement, she did not win it. She ran anyway. She won anyway, making her the first woman elected to the Senate without a widow or appointment connection. She was reelected to the Senate three more times.

Smith's watershed moment in the Senate was on June 1, 1950, when she took to the floor to criticize Senator Joseph McCarthy of Wisconsin for the smear tactics he used in his campaign against Communism. In her speech, which she later named a "Declaration of Conscience," she said:

> Those of us who shout the loudest about Americanism in making character assassinations are all too frequently those who, by our own words and acts, ignore some of the basic principles of Americanism—
>
> The right to criticize;
>
> The right to hold unpopular beliefs;
>
> The right to protest;
>
> The right of independent thought;
>
> The exercise of these rights should not cost one single American citizen his reputation or his right to a livelihood nor should he be in danger of losing his reputation or livelihood merely because he happens to know someone who holds unpopular beliefs. Who of us doesn't? Otherwise none of us could call our souls our own. Otherwise thought control would have set in.
>
> The American people are sick and tired of being afraid to speak their minds lest they be politically smeared as "Communists" or

"Fascists" by their opponents. Freedom of speech is not what it used to be in America. It has been so abused by some that it is not exercised by others.

Smith also accused McCarthy of debasing Senate deliberations "through the selfish political exploitation of fear, bigotry, ignorance and intolerance."

Sound like a problem we currently have with another elected male official? I thought so.

Smith definitely was not afraid to fight.

In 1964, eight years before Shirley Chisholm, Smith ran for the presidency, presenting and expressing the same courage and gutsiness she showed in 1950: "I have few illusions and no money, but I'm staying for the finish," she said. "When people keep telling you, you can't do a thing, you kind of like to try." At the Republican National Convention that year, she became the first woman to be considered by a major political party for nomination for the presidency.

Not afraid to fight for what's right—for a woman to be president.

At the time Smith ran for president, she had served in Congress for almost twenty-five years. But, like Clinton, her deep political experience didn't seem to matter. While she was regularly reelected to the legislature, when she sought executive office in the form of the presidency, her experience counted for little.

Like the other actions I encourage you to take in the campaign to elect our first woman president, being unafraid to fight takes courage. But remember that resisting and fighting for what's right for women can take many forms because there are many challenges to our equal rights and opportunities. Follow Smith and Chisholm, who fought the male political establishment in a time so much less conducive to women's attaining executive political power than ours. The least we can do is display similar courage as we fight, whenever and wherever we can.

YOUR ACTION PLAN: FIGHT

❏ **Talk about fighting for a woman president as if a woman president is a right, not a privilege.** In this manifesto, I couch our fight to elect our first woman president in the context of our nation's commitment to liberty and justice for all. We are not advocating any special treatment, only what is our due as Americans. Remember and assert this truth as you campaign.

❏ **Identify your fighter characteristics, and apply them to our campaign to elect our first woman president.** Women who fight for what's right share the attributes of courage, persistence, kindness, and conviction. However, the balance among these characteristics differs from one woman to another because each of us is unique. For instance, if you're comfortable debating (a popular form of fighting!), let her campaign know that. Not every woman is, so fight for her in that way.

❏ **Choose as role models women who have led politically.** These role models can be living or not. Their steadfast leadership example will sustain you and push you to keep fighting when you feel discouraged. Also, take heart from the role models whose stories I've told in this book. Considering any one of them and how she rose from defeat to victory will help prepare you for the fight we have on our hands today: electing Madam President.

❏ **Remember and act on the fact that when you choose to lead a fight, you set an example for others.** State's Attorney Kim Foxx reminded me that any woman who chooses to lead "sets the tone and culture" for those who follow her.

CHAPTER 19

I'M WITH HER

ACTION: BELIEVE

The marcher who created the sign that inspired this chapter—I'M WITH HER—borrowed Hillary Clinton's 2016 campaign slogan and, as you can see, applied it to the Statute of Liberty. "Her" refers to a robed figure of Libertas, the torchbearing Roman goddess who for thousands of years has symbolized freedom.

Early American revolutionary Thomas Paine wrote a poem titled "The Liberty Tree" in which this goddess of liberty brought to revolutionary era Boston the Liberty Tree, a symbol of the American Revolution. Her image was also prominent during the French Revolution, again to symbolize a fight for freedom from tyranny. Later, in the nineteenth century, a French sculptor imagined and created "her" to celebrate the centennial of the Declaration of Independence in 1876. Lady Liberty took her stand in New York Harbor in the 1880s, after much debate over finding a suitable location and raising funds to build a pedestal.

My favorite fact about the statue's history is this one, as reported in *Parade* magazine (emphasis mine): "When it was unveiled in October 1886, women's rights groups lamented that an enormous female figure would stand in New York Harbor representing liberty, *when most American women had no*

it's not about POLITICS. it's about BASIC HUMAN DECENCY.

—michelle obama

liberty to vote.... Suffragettes chartered a boat to circle the island during the unveiling. They blasted protest speeches."

Proverbially marching around the statute—much as we marched down streets in 2017 and again in 2018—our foremothers protested the irony of using a woman's image to represent liberty in a country where women were not free to vote. The irony haunts us: American men and women remain unequal, epitomized in the fact that, except as a statue, the torchbearer of the United States has never been a woman. We believe that our woman president will be that torchbearer—that "her" who represents liberty *for all.*

Nevertheless, the Statute of Liberty has symbolized the possibilities of American democracy and, for that reason, resonates for today's marchers, as it has for early American resisters and the immigrants seeking the freedom that the torchbearer represents.

Indeed, from 1892 to 1954, the Statue of Liberty welcomed more than 12 million immigrants who entered the United States through Ellis Island. One of those immigrants was my mother. A half century after she and her mother arrived at Ellis Island, I watched my mother make a move as though to kiss the ground after we returned from a trip to Michoacán, Mexico. My mother has never liked flying, but this gesture wasn't about feeling relieved after a safe plane landing. It *was* about her reverence for her adopted homeland, which she first experienced on the grounds of Ellis Island, adjacent to Liberty Island, the home of the Statue of Liberty. On an anniversary of her arrival at Ellis Island, she made a pilgrimage there with some of her children and grandchildren. (It's no wonder that her children are so patriotic!)

Of course, beliefs in such symbols can only be realized through actions, such as electing a woman who is our torchbearer, *for real.* Not until an American woman becomes president, looming as large over the nation and world as the Statue of Liberty does over New York Harbor—will every woman experience the ideas symbolized by Lady Liberty as reality.

These ideas are the same as those expressed in the Declaration of Independence, starting with "all men are created equal." When First Lady Michelle

Obama spoke at the 2016 Democratic National Convention, she made this clear: "I want a president who will teach our children that everyone in this country matters—a president who truly believes in the vision that our founders put forth all those years ago: that *we are all created equal,* each a beloved part of the great American story."

When I heard the First Lady say those words, I was reminded of the poem by Emma Lazarus that appears on the tablet held by Lady Liberty: "'Give me your tired, your poor, / Your huddled masses yearning to breathe free.'" I'm with her: let us all breathe free and make the symbolism of the Statue of Liberty true for every American.

YOUR ACTION PLAN: BELIEVE

❑ **Separate your political beliefs from your religious beliefs.** When you separate your belief in the importance of women's political power, rights, autonomy, and equality from *any* religious doctrine, you have a greater likelihood of winning support from others who don't share your religious beliefs. Don't let religion be a barrier to achieving political equality.

❑ **Support your beliefs with your actions.** Demonstrate your beliefs by undertaking specific actions. For instance, if you hear people making political arguments based on religious ideas, contest their statements to underscore the point that religious tenets aren't needed to legitimize political action. Then, propose actions that prove the point.

❑ **Develop arguments to counter non-factual statements.** In today's world of post-truth politics, people increasingly make statements based on what they believe to be true, or wish to be true, rather than on what is actually true. Sometimes these statements are outright lies. For instance, the *Washington Post* has documented Donald Trump's habit of telling lies as a way to convince voters that the truth is not really the truth. Such actions must be countered in the campaign to elect Madam President so that she isn't handicapped by naysayers because they believe these lies.

❑ **Seek out activist mentors who share your political beliefs.** These women and men will be your best guides, as they will be able to tell you how to be a grounded and influential activist. Further, these mentors will help you make your case because they are more experienced and better known. Therefore, they can express your beliefs in larger and likely more influential contexts than you can on your own.

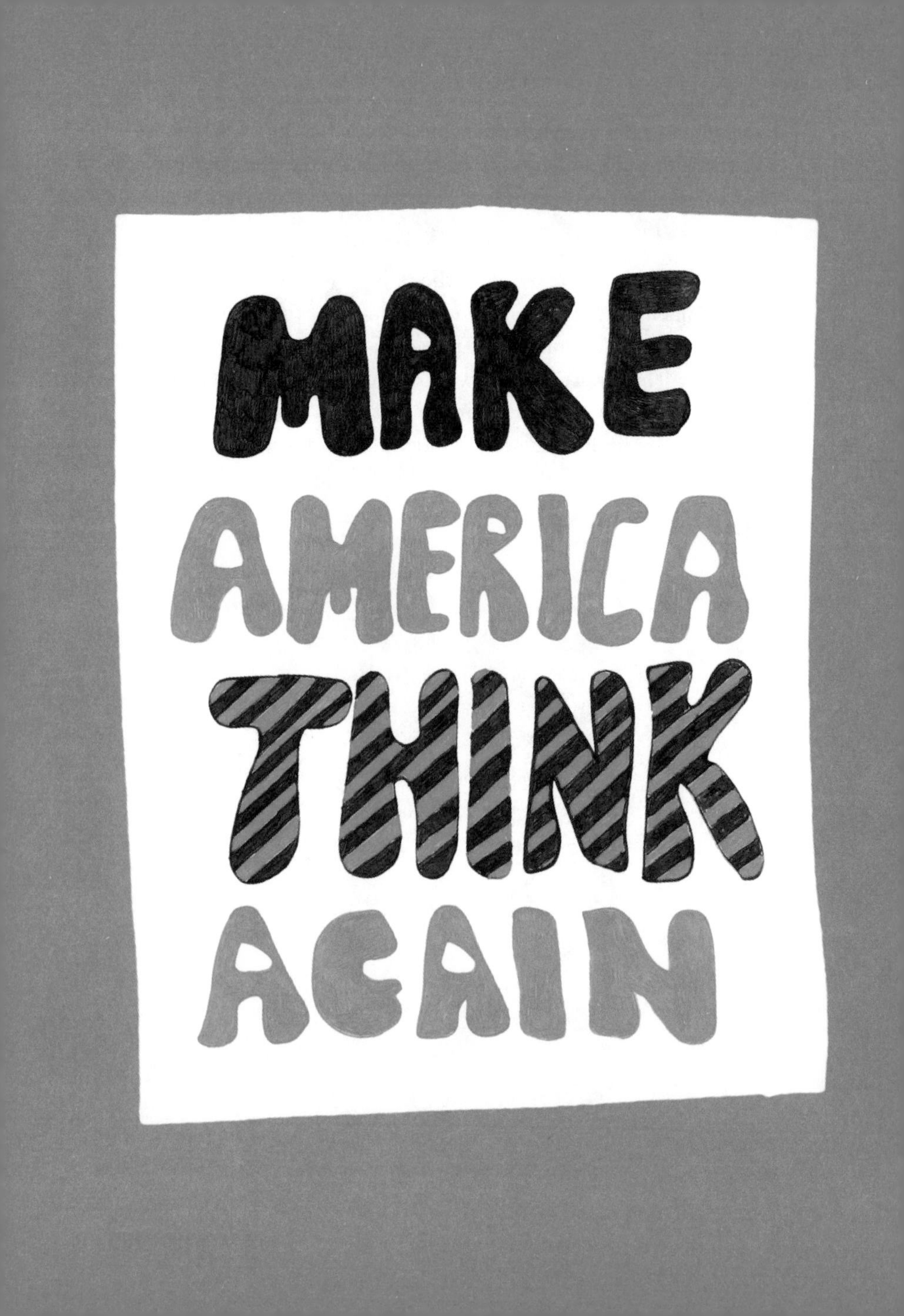
MAKE
AMERICA
THINK
AGAIN

CHAPTER 20

MAKE AMERICA THINK AGAIN

ACTION: EDUCATE

Every woman deserves to be educated about her self-interest in voting for a woman presidential candidate. Every woman should be asked to educate herself as much as she can, and then think about why electing Madam President is the best route for her to secure equality and opportunity for herself.

I do not mean that every woman needs a formal education in order to choose a presidential candidate. I *am* proposing better voter education efforts by those candidates' campaigns so that each voter fully thinks about her choices and uses her knowledge in her presidential vote. This type of education should be front and center in our campaign planning to elect our first woman president.

Tragically, this goal was not achieved in the 2016 presidential election, when factors of race, culture, income, and level of education divided women voters—to their great detriment. Some posit that the ways women voted in 2016 were driven by income level and partnership status with a man: the lower a woman's income, the more reliant she is on her partner's income, and if that partner is a man, that meant she likely voted like him (which largely translated to voting for Donald Trump if that partner was a white man). Others have written that the explanation for women voting against their gender and class interests by voting for Trump—a candidate who promised to solve women's economic insecurity but didn't present any realistic plan for doing so—was their belief that the government itself was what most needed changing, and Trump said he would change that. At the same time, among white women, the more formal education a woman had, the more likely it was she voted for Hillary Clinton—there was a 20-point gender gap between the voting of college-educated and non-college-educated white women (56 percent to 36 percent, respectively).

However these data are interpreted, the tragic result was that a majority of white women voters did not vote for Hillary Clinton, the candidate whose policy proposals would have been most beneficial to them (as they would have been to every woman). Marchers knew this. One response was MAKE AMERICA THINK AGAIN, a clever play on Trump's campaign slogan that points out that if women voters had been better educated about the implications of each candidate's policy proposals, more of them would have voted for Clinton.

This gap between women's interests and women's votes must be closed with a smarter voter education program if our first woman president is to be elected anytime soon. No woman needs a formal education to understand the advantages of being a self-interested voter, but every woman does deserve as compelling a case as possible for her consideration.

In a commentary piece for the *Chicago Tribune*, Renee Elliott, who lost her job at the Indianapolis Carrier factory that Donald Trump promised to save, spoke to the tragedy of believing Trump's rhetoric:

> Last month, despite Trump's promise, Carrier laid off another 215 employees and shifted their work to Mexico. I lost my job. As a result, I'm losing my health insurance, my retirement benefits and quite possibly my home. . . . I feel betrayed, angry and forgotten—and I'm not alone. . . . Even though working people like me helped put Trump in the White House, the truth is that he's done nothing to keep his promises to save American jobs.

As Elliott pointed out, any objective examination of Trump's policy proposals and endorsed legislation would conclude that his legislative record to date has not been good for working people. His tax cuts favor the wealthy. His lack of commitment to children's health care—as evidenced by his utter disinterest in renewing the Children's Health Insurance Program, which helps low-income children—and his efforts to repeal the Affordable Care Act, which enables every woman to access essential health services, including reproductive health care services, reveal his lack of concern for working women and their families. The action I propose here is to make America think again, which starts with finding ways to educate voters about why it is important to vote in their self-interest.

Signs indicate a movement of white women voters away from Donald Trump and like-minded candidates in favor of progressive Democrats who support public policies that help women achieve economic security. Recent electoral victories in Virginia, Alabama, and Wisconsin suggest that both male and female voters are thinking smarter about policy proposals and not being swayed by empty rhetoric. A Washington Post–ABC poll from early 2018 found that just 37 percent of white women approved of Trump's job performance in January 2018, down from 47 percent in April 2017. Of those without a college degree (an important demographic for Trump), just 43 percent approved of his job performance. This trend holds true for women with college degrees as well—while 40 percent said they approved of Trump's performance in April 2017, just 27 percent did so in January 2018. Since then, women's views of Trump have continued to deteriorate.

Even though white women are starting to shift away from Trump, we can't ignore the fact that a racial divide persists among voters, as the 2016 presidential election revealed so starkly. Fifty-seven percent of white voters chose Trump in 2016, compared to just 8 percent of black voters. Conversely, 37 percent of white voters chose Clinton, while 89 percent of black voters did. Race continues to factor into American politics in the most invidious of ways.

Even the women's suffrage movement experienced a racial divide, as many white suffragists did not support black women getting the vote. In 1867,

Sojourner Truth called for unity across *gender* lines to demand suffrage for all women, in the same way that women today must unify across gender and racial lines to elect our first woman president:

> I feel that I have the right to have just as much as a man. There is a great stir about colored men getting their rights, but not a word about the colored women; and if colored men get their rights, and not colored women theirs, the colored men will be masters over the women, and it will be just as bad as it was before.

Former Planned Parenthood President Cecile Richards said at the 2018 Women's March #PowertothePolls rally in Las Vegas, "So white women, listen up. We've got to do better. It is not up to women of color to save this country from itself. That's on all of us. That's on all of us."

But we don't have to convince every woman voter to select our prospective Madam President, who will likely work hard to save this country from itself. The task *is* to educate enough of them who weren't convinced in 2016. Thankfully, in our campaign to elect our first woman president, this may require victory in only a few more states, for instance in those midwestern states that Trump won by small margins. No matter. A win is a win. *Yes, she can* will be truth.

This voter education campaign could start with college-educated white women who voted for Donald Trump because that group of voters was more likely to vote for Clinton than their non-college-educated white sisters. While these women may not have great job security either and, like their lower-income sisters, likely earn less than their male counterparts, they might be the most receptive to this campaign because they know how important federal economic policy is to their professional advancement. The *New York Times*, in a lead article on February 3, 2018, discussed the prospect of significant state legislative victories in 2018 and noted that Republican "dominance appears to be fraying . . . especially in areas around major cities where President Trump has stirred an insurrection among liberals, and college-educated voters and white women have recoiled from Republicans."

I live part-time in rural Michigan. While helping me pull weeds in the summer before the 2016 presidential election, a friend of mine, a non-college-educated white woman, told me that the increase in her health insurance premium under the Affordable Care Act would make her more likely to vote for the Republican candidate. (This was before Donald Trump was nominated. I have not asked her how she voted.) Her health insurance premium had been significantly less under the old system when she could purchase an individual plan with a high but manageable deductible. According to her, no similar plan was offered in Michigan after the passage of the Affordable Care Act.

She believed her premium rose because of the ACA's required subsidies for low-income people.

While some of the changes in coverage my friend experienced were likely a result of actions by the state of Michigan, she apparently *was* worse off as a result of the federal bill. There was no mistaking her sense of hurt. She talked about how much she was suffering, even though she worked hard and was a responsible employer and employee. She shared how unfair she thought it was that even with these qualities, she was still suffering. I left the conversation wishing she were old enough for Medicare because it would, at least in some part, cure her problem. But that's not enough: a better voter education program in Michigan might have been.

Several months later, I talked with my friend's aunt, also not college-educated, about the job situation in our area of rural Michigan. "There are no jobs here," she told me, as we discussed the fact there once were many more in manufacturing, for instance at nearby Whirlpool, which has moved much of its manufacturing abroad.

These two smart women identified two policy arenas of life-saving importance to every woman: health care and jobs. I don't know how they voted in 2016, but I do know this: they want the same economic security that I, a college-educated woman, do. The remedy here is, as marchers put it, to MAKE AMERICA SMART AGAIN by educating every voter about the importance to her own life of supporting candidates who propose economic policies that advance economic security for *every woman*, even when other policy proposals may be distasteful.

Senator Bernie Sanders's policy proposals for economic reform prevailed in the 2016 Michigan Democratic primary when he bested Clinton. The Michiganders who voted for him were onto something. Months later, Clinton learned her Michigan campaign was in trouble, so she led a rally in Grand Rapids the day before the general election. Until then, she hadn't appeared in western Michigan, the home of my friends in pain. Apparently, neither Clinton nor her staffers had been thinking smartly enough about the voter education program these women voters deserved. A rally wasn't going to suffice, and it didn't. Clinton lost Michigan the next day.

Let's build the new voter education campaign every woman deserves. This campaign will prove that every woman is in this fight with every other woman.

YOUR ACTION PLAN: EDUCATE

❑ **Create voter education activities for your neighborhood organization.** If you aren't yet a member of a neighborhood organization, join one that focuses on an issue or issues of concern to you. It is likely that voter education will be useful to its members, and because many neighborhood activists are women, your pro-Madam President message will likely be received enthusiastically.

❑ **Partner your organization with other women's and girls' organizations to advocate women's public leadership.** This will give you the opportunity to educate women beyond your immediate circle about the value of electing Madam President.

❑ **Educate your family about why the election of our first woman president will improve their lives.** One of the benefits of taking on this responsibility is that you will learn what arguments are persuasive for what types of people. Remember the information you learn, and share it with friends who are educating *their* families.

❑ **Educate your friends about the importance of electing Madam President.** Make sure your friends, regardless of what their past voting choices have been, understand why electing our first woman president is likely to improve their personal *and* work lives. To do this, share the policy proposals of Madam President's campaign, providing clear examples of how, if implemented, these proposals will benefit them, their families, and their friends. Remember as you do this that the margin of victory can be tiny, so every persuaded voter counts.

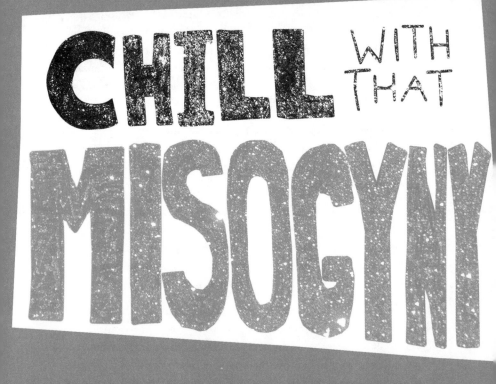

CHAPTER 21

WORDS MATTER

ACTION: WRITE

Among all of the marchers' words that have helped frame this book, one poster from the 2017 Chicago Women's March is a favorite of mine: CHILL WITH THAT MISOGYNY. The word *misogyny* is defined as "a hatred of women." That's it, folks. The poster was proudly displayed by an African American woman and a young girl who might have been her daughter. The woman was wearing a black T-shirt proclaiming *Nasty Women.*

Another one of my favorite posters read WORDS MATTER and was held by a woman standing next to her woman friend wearing a pussy-hat-pink T-shirt with the words *Planned Parenthood* in bold white lettering across it. Indeed, they do. They frame our thinking about what matters in our lives and guide the actions we can take to realize what matters.

Earlier in this book, I wrote about the first project of my feminist organizing career, the *Chicago Women's Directory / Guía para las Mujeres de Chicago.* I organized a group of friends to write and publish the book. We named our collective Inforwomen (get it?) and got to work (1970s feminism was big on collective decision making—what fun that was). However, I didn't mention earlier why I chose to initiate the project and organize the group while working as a file clerk, attending graduate school, giving visitor tours of Hull-House, and learning about being married and living in a new city! It was because I knew words matter.

The summer before my husband and I moved to Chicago, we lived and worked in Cambridge, Massachusetts. There, I read two books that made an indelible impression on me: *Our Bodies, Ourselves*, a booklet on women's health written by the Boston Women's Health Book Collective, and the *Women's Yellow Pages*, a guide to community services.

I had lived in Chicago the prior year, when I had attended an off-campus semester for political science students. The women's movement was blooming in Chicago, but I had not seen any publications like these. When my husband and I arrived in Chicago, I learned there were still no similar publications. I decided I would organize a group to write the Chicago version of the *Women's Yellow Pages*. I knew those kinds of words would matter as much in Chicago as they had in Boston. Reading those words, Chicago women would be energized as well as informed. Therefore, the directory's list of health clinics was accompanied by an essay that began as follows:

> The issue of women's health is a vital one, covering many areas of concern to all women regardless of class or race. . . . The control of our bodies is a necessary step towards the control of our lives politically. . . . We must all become more aware of the important roles we can have in changing the health care system; roles in which our feminist beliefs in the capabilities and potential of women can have real substance and meaning.

The directory was published in English and Spanish, the latter also a first language of many Chicagoans.

Another book circulating then that had a profound effect on me was *What Is to Be Done? Burning Questions of Our Movement*, written in 1901 by Vladimir Lenin, political philosopher and organizer, founder of the Communist Party of the Soviet Union, and leader of the 1917 October Revolution, which

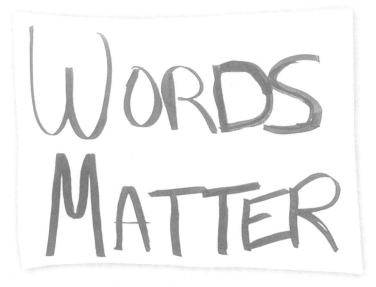

led to the Communist takeover of the Russian government. In it, I found this passage (emphasis mine):

> Class political consciousness can't be brought to the workers *only from without:* that is, only from outside the sphere of relations between workers and employers. The sphere from which alone it is possible to obtain this knowledge is the sphere of relationships of *all* classes and strata to the state and the government, the sphere of the interrelations between *all* classes.

I read Lenin's words to mean that women, too, needed to determine their relationship to one another, regardless of class, as well as to government, and then needed to promote government policies that enforced equitable treatment of women. These words were important, even in light (or dark) of the human rights horrors that followed.

The greatest presidential inaugural addresses, State of the Union speeches, candidate speeches, political manifestos, and march posters—whatever the march—use words to evoke deep sentiments and political mobilization among those who hear or read or see them.

One powerful example of such words is in President John F. Kennedy's inaugural address in January 1961, when he declared, "Ask not what your country can do for you—ask what you can do for your country." I was remembering that Inauguration Day recently in a conversation with my mother, and she reminded me that school had been closed that day due to heavy snowfall. Our family had gathered in the basement in front of the television to watch Kennedy's speech. Inspired for years afterward, as millions of other American children were, I became interested in joining the Peace Corps. Instead, I joined the women's movement and started writing. I had learned that words matter.

The words of ordinary people can be just as significant as those of the powerful. Consider the iconic I AM A MAN posters made and carried by African American male sanitation workers during Dr. Martin Luther King Jr.'s last march in Memphis, Tennessee, in 1968, when he was killed because of hatred for his words and his courageous acts stemming from them. At many times in American history, words have been so powerful that they mobilized a movement, not merely a political campaign. That's what electing an African American president in 2008 was: the victory of a movement. Barack Obama made that clear when he quoted labor organizer Dolores Huerta's words, "Sí, se puede," to describe the purpose of the campaign. Yes, we can. Those words did it.

Today we say *these* words for *our* American revolution: "Yes, *she* can."

YOUR ACTION PLAN: WRITE

❏ **Assert your opinion in writing, frequently.** Assert your opinion about the importance of electing a woman president in every written context you can create for yourself. This could be in letters to the editor or opinion columns in your local newspaper, in blog posts, on your organization's website or in its newsletter, or, as I've already suggested, in speeches you write or comments you make at neighborhood or campaign meetings.

❏ **Encourage every woman you know to write, too.** The more written advocacy for women's rights and electing Madam President, the better off our campaign to elect her will be. That's because more and more women will then know the importance of having her in our lives. And, as more and more women write, that will embolden other women to write, too. The circle will keep widening and deepening and, before you know it, there will be enough women voting to elect Madam President. What a glorious day that will be!

❏ **Share all of this writing as often as you can with as many as you can.** Luckily for us, almost every woman today owns her own printing press in the form of her social media accounts. Use them for this purpose, please!

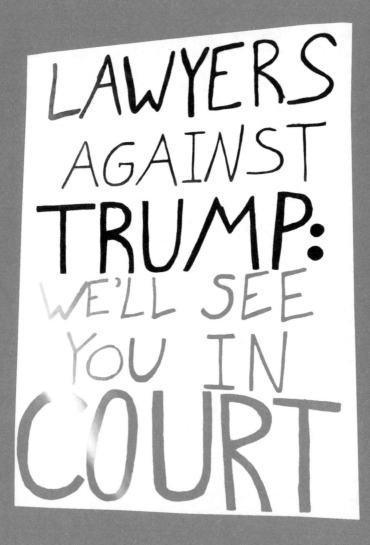

CHAPTER 22

WE'LL SEE YOU IN COURT

ACTION: LITIGATE

O ne of the most dramatic acts we can take to advance women's equality and opportunity to run for political office is to have our lawyers go to court to defend and advance our legal and political rights. As the marcher whose poster's message inspired this chapter said, when our lawyers go to court, we are all saying, WE'LL SEE YOU IN COURT, and we're willing to go there, too, to fight for our rights. And while the lawyers among us will be the ones representing us in court, the rest of us can take other actions to support their work.

Notorious RBG, aka Supreme Court Justice Ruth Bader Ginsburg, and my father, David Sive, served on the executive committee of the New York City Bar Association in the early 1970s, when Ginsburg chaired its Special Committee on Sex and the Law. I met her in the late 1970s, thanks to my father's introduction. While teaching at Rutgers Law School, Ginsburg had cofounded the *Women's Rights Law Reporter*, the first such journal in the nation. She then moved to Columbia Law School and became the founding director of the American Civil Liberties Union (ACLU) Women's Rights Project, which goes to court to defend and expand women's legal rights.

By then, Ginsburg was already notorious (in a good way) to the likes of me for her steadfast and groundbreaking advocacy of women's rights, and she has remained ever present in my mind as I work for women's rights.

Increasingly, I hold her in my heart with gratefulness for everything she has done for women.

In 2013, when Supreme Court Justice Sonia Sotomayor lectured in Chicago after her autobiography, *My Beloved World,* was published, she told the audience that at the celebration of Supreme Court Justice Elena Kagan's appointment, President Barack Obama leaned over to give Justice Ginsburg a kiss and whispered in her ear, "Are you happy I gave you two sisters?" According to Sotomayor, Ginsburg replied, "I will be happy when you bring me five more."

As a feminist, and only the second woman appointed to the Supreme Court (mind you, that appointment, made by President Bill Clinton, was only in 1993), one of only four women justices to ever serve on the Supreme Court, Justice Ginsburg's opinions, whether majority or dissenting, have shaped every American woman's treatment under the law. In doing so, she has laid the groundwork for our campaign to elect—as our first Madam President—a woman who will be able to advocate for more laws and court decisions that benefit women and recognize the full possibilities of women's rights under the Constitution.

Marchers recognized this truth about Ginsburg's unique contributions and, consequently, expressed their belief that more women like her on the Supreme Court would be good for women. One marcher held a sign that asked HOW MANY WOMEN SHOULD BE ON THE SUPREME COURT?, referencing Ginsburg's comment to President Obama. They also recognized, through consideration of her decisions, the importance to all women of the judiciary, whether federal, state, or local. Another poster—KEEP YOUR LAWS OFF MY DRAWERS (*drawers* meaning "underpants")—went to the heart of one key, courts-related matter: women's reproductive decision making.

When Shana Knizhnik, then a New York University law student, created the Notorious RBG Tumblr, my fangirl mode came full circle. So what if I had never become a lawyer, my father's dream for me? I could still be a fangirl of the lawyer I would have wanted to become: one notorious for her unwavering

We'll See You in Court | 171

commitment to women's rights. I could still try to follow in Notorious RBG's footsteps, albeit in another profession, trying to be as stalwart as she is in speaking out and dissenting when necessary, always in favor of advancing equality.

An essential attribute of the Madam President we will elect is the courage and confidence to act singularly. It is in this context that Ginsburg and her predecessor, Sandra Day O'Connor, who was the lone woman on the US Supreme Court for twelve years, are unique role models. With the stroke of a pen, these women have made laws. At times, they wrote as lone dissenters showing the way forward for future legislation or court arguments and decisions. Madam President will be able to be just as courageous and singular in her advocacy—and so can we as we campaign to elect her.

As we do, we must bear in mind that the federal court system has a unique role in our system of government. The US Supreme Court is our last stop on the path to justice—yet another reason why electing Madam President matters so much, as she will appoint those justices.

Consider the subject matter of some early US Supreme Court victories for women's rights—almost all of which were decided since Ginsburg founded the ACLU Women's Rights Project. My mind boggled as I read the ACLU's "Timeline of Major Supreme Court Decisions on Women's Rights." At first, I thought I could share the entire almost half century of highlights with you, but there are too many, demonstrating my point of why it is so important to be willing to go to court.

The following rights affecting all aspects of women's lives have been secured in Supreme Court decisions:

- Women with young children must be hired if a similarly situated man would be.
- Abortion is constitutionally protected.
- Unmarried people can obtain contraception.

- Female and male workers doing the same job must be paid the same wage.
- States must call men and women to jury service on an equal basis.
- Social Security survivor benefits must be paid without sex-based distinctions or assumptions of dependency.

Notorious RBG has had no fear—ever—of singular acts, as evidenced by her many dissenting Supreme Court decisions. She has not feared lone dissents either. Ginsburg has a "'dissent' collar," a white lace collar that complements her black robe (you can see it pictured in the illustration on page 171), which she wears on days when she presents a dissenting opinion. She also appeared to be wearing it the day after Donald Trump's election.

Ginsburg's dissenting opinion in the 2014 *Burwell v. Hobby Lobby Stores* case—in which she was joined by the other two women justices, Sotomayor and Kagan—made clear the need for women's voices on the Supreme Court. The all-male majority opinion stated that closely held corporations have the right to cite their religious beliefs as a reason to refuse to provide their employees with insurance coverage for birth control. Ginsburg plainly stated the problem with the majority's view: "The exemption sought by Hobby Lobby and Conestoga would . . . deny legions of women who do not hold their employers' beliefs access to contraceptive coverage that the ACA would otherwise secure."

Period. End of sentence.

As the marcher said, see you in court.

YOUR ACTION PLAN: LITIGATE

❑ **Educate yourself on women's legal issues so that you can propose court action when needed.** As you educate yourself, also educate others, so that the voices and actions of women's legal rights proponents are loud and clear. Keep in mind that hurtful legal action comes in a variety of forms and from all three branches of government. Consequently, you'll need to keep track of judicial decisions and executive orders as well as harmful legislation. Though this may sound like an overwhelming task, it is not. Educate yourself on the issues that matter most to you and the organizations you are involved in. Ask your friends involved in other causes to educate you about those. Together, pay attention to the issues prioritized by Madam President's campaign so that you can be an advocate there, too.

❑ **Be an activist in contexts that advance women's legal rights.** There are many contexts in which you can support and promote women's legal rights, as well as take legal action to preserve or expand them. For instance, you can help build support for the lawyers who handle such matters and the officials who propose legal remedies, such as new legislation. Support and promotion can be organizing public actions such as marches to draw attention to the issue and the solution you propose. Or it can be a media campaign to advance public understanding of the problem you identify. Or it can be encouraging your friends to speak out and defend the cause. The goal here is to do everything you can to make sure the fight to secure women's legal rights is not hobbled by inaction.

❑ **Support women lawyers who work in the public interest. Give them your money and your time.** Many of the lawsuits you will be concerned about are brought by public interest organizations. These organizations rely on the support of people like us to fund their work.

Your making a financial commitment and asking others to do the same is very valuable. Don't wait to be asked—if you read about a lawsuit in your local paper or a coworker tells you about one or a friend shares her story, act on that information and offer your support in every way that you can.

❏ **Support the young women you meet who want to become public interest lawyers. One of them might become Madam President one day!** As you help these women, remember that women lawyers frequently decide to run for office. A common route is beginning with legislative office and then seeking executive office. Attorney General Lisa Madigan is a good example. She started as a state senator and then became Illinois attorney general. That's the kind of executive political knowledge and power that positions women to run for the presidency. So help young women pursue their dreams by supporting them in every way you can.

❏ **Advocate for women lawyers situated to seek elected executive office or rise in appointed executive governmental positions.** Your reasons for this advocacy are straightforward: the earlier women can demonstrate their executive decision-making and policy-making skills, the sooner they can start climbing the ladder to greater executive governmental power and the farther they can ultimately climb. You can promote these women by getting involved in their political campaigns, telling others why you are enthusiastic about their candidacies, or helping them raise money. If the woman you support is seeking appointive office, you can lobby people you know, people you meet, or people whom your friends or colleagues know who can recommend her selection.

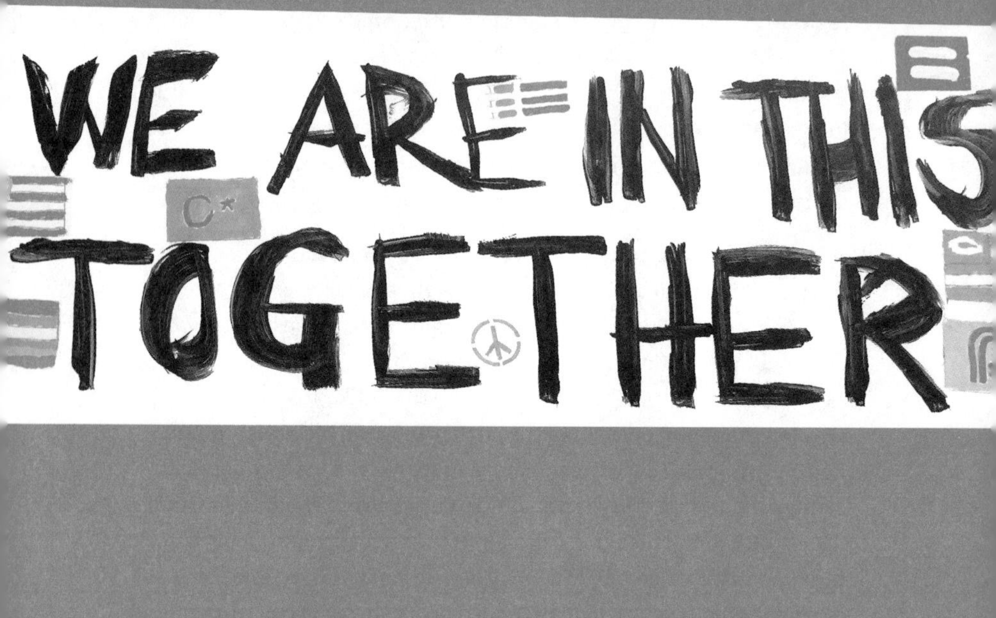
WE ARE IN THIS
TOGETHER

CHAPTER 23

WE ARE IN THIS TOGETHER

ACTION: ELECT YOURSELF

In the campaign to elect our first woman president, you can elect yourself, too. If you become deeply engaged in the campaign to elect Madam President, which I hope I have convinced you to do, you will learn about the political process and what it takes to win politically. You will have firsthand knowledge of and experience with campaign actions, including what they require of the candidate and how it feels to engage in them. You can then assess what you have learned and reconcile it with your own ambitions. Why not elect yourself? *Our country needs you, too.*

Several years ago, I wrote a handbook for women who want to run for office. In it, I shared the strategies of gifted women leaders all over the nation, as well as from my own lifetime of public leadership and helping women become leaders in the public square. Appropriately, its very title, *Every Day Is Election Day: A Woman's Guide to Winning Any Office, from the PTA to the White House*, posed the idea of a woman running for president. Clearly, this would be the ultimate Election Day for American women.

I had decided to write *Every Day Is Election Day* after the 2008 Democratic presidential primary. Out of necessity, it was forthright, as well as ambitious. Hillary Clinton had just run against (and lost to) Barack Obama.

Her loss meant that running a winning presidential campaign for a woman remained the goal for those who believed it was time to vote her in.

It was clear after that primary that for women presidential candidates, being qualified was just not enough. At that point, Clinton had more governmental experience than Obama did. As First Lady for eight years, during which she championed myriad causes and policies benefiting women, girls, and families, Clinton had gained an insider's knowledge and experience of the White House and congressional policy making. Subsequently, she had served for eight years as a US senator from New York. By contrast, at that point, Obama had served as an Illinois state senator for seven years and as a US senator for less than four years. Seemingly, maleness trumped experience: the public preferred a less experienced man to a more experienced woman.

While Obama's election to the presidency brought tears of joy to my eyes and the eyes of everyone I know, there remained another obstacle to surmount: electing a woman president. "Fired up! Ready to go!" as Obama said so often in his 2008 presidential campaign, would be our motto, henceforth.

Every Day Is Election Day boldly asserts what I have also asserted here: that women deserve and should aggressively seek executive political and governmental power. It proposes confronting those who might get in a woman's way. In fact, it recommends challenging authority every step of the way, as American political authority is still overwhelmingly male, and the men who possess it typically seek to preserve their prerogatives and domains.

Every Day Is Election Day promotes campaigning to get to the head of the line as fast as possible, not by stepping on or over anyone else but by working harder and faster. It argues that succeeding as a woman in a man's world (politics) requires supporting women—not pretending that women and men have such similar needs and challenges that paying special attention to women (and the public policies that benefit them) isn't needed. It calls for dreaming and planning big, because most women I have met in public life are willing to do the work and accept the responsibility that comes with political power.

Obviously, these guidelines are all about electing our first woman president—guidelines for the women who will seek that role now that Clinton has improved the odds of a woman winning that race. And if you decide to elect yourself, these guidelines are for you, too.

I have no doubt that achieving your own political ambitions will help the campaign to elect our first woman president. Once you become a leader, you will have more power and influence over others. You will also know more about politics and governance because you will have been encouraging others to participate in this campaign of ours. And you will know a lot more about the personal qualities and skills needed to be an effective political leader. Why not utilize that knowledge to continue to advance yourself so you can help others lead better lives?

As part of my research for this book, as I have mentioned, I interviewed three friends who have executive governmental power now: Lisa Madigan, Illinois attorney general; Kimberly (Kim) M. Foxx, Cook County, Illinois, state's attorney; and Anna Valencia, city clerk of Chicago. I think their action plan for electing yourself is particularly instructive.

As you review their advice, remember this wise counsel from Attorney General Madigan: be *deeply* appreciative of the women who have marked this way for you. Once a woman runs—and especially if she wins—she opens the door to other women's candidacies. So, with that in mind, start every day of your action plan with gratefulness.

YOUR ACTION PLAN: ELECT YOURSELF

❑ **Remember that you "own your own destiny" as a political leader, and integral to that destiny is remaining committed to helping women and girls.** No matter how often you may consult with others in your decision making or how open-minded you are to others' ideas, you are the final decision maker about your political future. While others may disagree with your decision, you have the sole responsibility to decide what office you want to seek and, if you win it, how you will execute its responsibilities. If you lose, you still have the sole responsibility to decide your future path.

In this context, State's Attorney Foxx pointed out the importance of local office. "There is so much we can do on the local level to benefit women," she said. At the same time, she pointed out that local office-holders are important advocates against "federal policy that is obstructionist to women." Her bottom line: if you feel your destiny is local office, go for it. And if you subsequently decide to seek higher office, go for that, too. Just make sure that your prospective female constituents will benefit from your policy choices.

As examples of local policies that matter to every woman, State's Attorney Foxx mentioned those regarding paid sick leave, minimum wage laws, and access to reproductive health services. She also mentioned decisions about hiring and promoting women; handling allegations of sexual harassment; and making sure that the workplace is conducive to mothers, for example, to those breast-feeding newborns and those with school-age children. She told me that some women she knew weren't returning to work after their maternity leave because their workplaces were inhospitable to new mothers. She also mentioned that some fathers who took paternity leave had been mocked, prompting her to foster a better workplace understanding of the roles of parents. Now that a US senator has given birth while in office and voted from the Senate floor, baby in arms, there is once again proof of the benefits of creating policies that reflect the fact that mothers are in the workplace.

❑ **Listen to your inner voice for guidance.** Executives are expected to make decisions quickly and with confidence. When you do, listen to yourself to make sure you are headed in the direction that makes the most sense to you. If others perceive your decision as pushing a particular agenda, Clerk Valencia recommended saying, "That's right, and here is why my agenda makes sense." Then be prepared to defend your position, which should be forceful because you are heeding your inner voice (as Clerk Valencia also recommended).

❑ **Make sure male superiors support your decisions and that you aren't evaluated on different criteria from those applied to your male coworkers.** Even if you're in an executive governmental position, you may report to a man, particularly if your position is an appointed one. Make sure he will stand by you, and if you sense that he won't, negotiate a new understanding with him so that you maintain your authority.

Like male leaders, women leaders make mistakes. If you do, don't let your boss, the public, the media, or voters hold you (or any other woman officeholder or candidate) to an unattainable standard or to one that is different from the standard applied to your male coworkers or competitors. Otherwise you won't be able to do your job in the way you should and in the way your constituents need. After all, that is your ultimate responsibility, while never acceding to sexist decision making.

❑ **Never forget that when you hold public office, you are a role model.** Every woman in politics or government is a role model, but because political and governmental women executives are still so rare, prepare yourself to be an important role model for other women and girls who seek such roles. In this context, Attorney General Madigan noted that if you hold such a position, you will often be held up as an example by mothers whose daughters have ambitions like yours. Be prepared for those experiences, and welcome those conversations. State's Attorney Foxx also underscored the importance of being a role model: "There is the symbolic piece: I see it, so I can be it."

❑ **Seek out other women political leaders for guidance, and consider carefully what they have to say.** You might be the first woman in your jurisdiction to run for your executive position, as was the case with Attorney General Madigan, or the first single woman, or the first woman without children, or the first out lesbian. In such important circumstances, remember that while there may be no other woman in your circle or political community who holds a similar office, there are likely others around the country who do. They can offer you sound advice for succeeding on the job. Seek them out, listen carefully to their advice, and then follow it.

❑ **Network with other women leaders for support and guidance.** This advice from Clerk Valencia applies during the good times but is especially useful during the bad ones. She recommends that when you feel outnumbered or as though you don't belong, seek reassurance and guidance from other women leaders, whether they are leaders in government or in some other institution. Those women are your peer group and can give you the forthright guidance you need.

Clerk Valencia also mentioned that, depending on your background, you may never have met or even observed a woman with power or public leadership responsibilities and therefore have no contextual framework for how women successfully seek and hold such positions. She told me she was such a woman, having grown up in a working-class family in a small town. Soon after her appointment to city clerk, she sought the support and advice of other women executives in Chicago. They continue to meet monthly.

❑ **Determine your brand.** Your brand is your political identity, informed by your primary message. Think about the example of Shirley Chisholm that I shared with you earlier: her brand was independence, expressed in her message, "unbought and unbossed." Branding is best done at the outset of your campaign and then confirmed upon election. But, no matter what else you may say about yourself, your branding message should reflect your commitment to advancing women in politics and government and securing women's rights and opportunities. Clerk Valencia noted that if this commitment to women and their causes was not sufficiently evident previously, make sure that it is once you're in charge.

❑ **Guard your privacy, but don't deny your personality or life choices.** Clerk Valencia advised both being true to yourself *and* staying "closely guarded" in order to prevent untoward questions from the public. She said some people have told her she doesn't seem motherly or grandmotherly, as though those characteristics are required for all women leaders. She told me she "calls people out" when they make such erroneous statements.

❑ **Don't ever let the job go to your head.** Attorney General Madigan told me she walks out of her office regularly during the course of the day. "I go and gather information," she said. "I'm happy to walk down the hall and meet wherever. It's about getting the job done, not about my own ego."

❑ **There can never be too many women in charge.** Remember that if you promote women to positions they haven't previously held and someone says, "There are too many women now," remind him (most likely, the complainer will be a "him") that it's likely no one ever said that when men predominated in such positions. State's Attorney Foxx said she has started assigning more women to complex litigation matters not only because it is the right course of action but also to demonstrate that women should hold every job, just as their male counterparts have.

❑ **Resist being "gender neutral."** Neutrality isn't the goal. State's Attorney Foxx made a really important point when she said, "When we have gender-neutral conversations, we leave women behind. The norm is not men; it is everybody." Continuing, she emphasized that women leaders have a unique opportunity to "change the workplace culture and make sure women's voices are heard." She advised not to ever fear saying, "I see the world through the eyes of being a woman."

State's Attorney Foxx characterized this approach as useful when considering the correct criminal charge in a case where a woman victim of domestic violence is charged with murder, or deciding how to proceed in a he-said, she-said case of sexual assault, or responding to (male) prosecutors who say that being charged with rape is so horrible that a rapist just shouldn't be charged!

State's Attorney Foxx also encouraged helping younger women recognize sexist behavior and determine how best to address it.

❑ **Ask for what you want, including more women leaders (including yourself).** "We should never be afraid to ask for what we want," Clerk Valencia said. "If I hadn't lobbied, I probably wouldn't have gotten the positions I wanted." Once you get the job you want, Attorney General Madigan said, be committed to driving hard bargains in order to create meaningful solutions for your constituents, rather than, say, solving a momentary problem that enables you to emerge as a temporary victor.

While you lobby for yourself, lobby for other women to become leaders and candidates, too. You don't have to support every woman running for office just because she is a woman, however. Instead, your criteria for whether or not to support a candidate should be whether that candidate shares your belief in women's right to political and governmental leadership, including the presidency.

As you can conclude from considering all this good advice, we are all in this work together, including how and when to elect Madame President. And today's numbers of politically motivated women underscore the possibility of achieving this victory soon. EMILY's List announced in early 2018 that since the 2016 election, more than 34,000 women had expressed interest in running for office. A remarkable poll conducted in 2018 by VoteRunLead and Bustle Trends Group found that 15 percent of the women surveyed said they plan to run for office in 2018 or in the future!

I have no doubt that, as these tens of thousands of women decide to run and as hundreds of thousands of us continue to resist and to promote women's political equality and governmental leadership, we can act on this manifesto's proposal *together*. Let's work to elect Madam President so that it is clear once and for all that American women can run and govern *anything* and *everything*.

Women
Together
Forward

CONCLUSION WOMEN TOGETHER FORWARD

I have argued in this manifesto that the reason we should all be in this campaign to elect Madam President together is because her election will prove that American women can move forward as one politically while making the world better for every woman. Further, I have argued that a woman at the apex of our nation's commitment to life, liberty, and equal justice for all—and at the apex of the world's decision making—will change the entire world's view of what women can do and illustrate why women executives in government and politics are good for everyone.

I hope I have made it clear why *this* campaign is *the right one for right now* and how this campaign is doable *by all of us now*. I have written that this campaign will be revolutionary in its impact for those of us who:

- Marched in January 2017
- Marched again in January 2018
- Keep marching for any cause benefiting women and girls
- Work to elect women candidates
- Lobby public officials to do right by women
- Teach our girls they can be anything, even president

One of my favorite Women's March posters boldly captures an admittedly irreverent statement of this manifesto's mission: WOMEN TOGETHER FORWARD, with initial caps in bold, pussy-hat-pink letters reading "WTF," or "What the fuck?"

While this term isn't one I use, I agree with its sentiment. American women have been shut out of the Oval Office for far too long, not to mention shut out of other positions of executive governmental power, including those that are stepping-stones to the presidency. While 2018 has been named another "Year of the Woman"—and it is in terms of the record numbers of women either running or training to run for office—I want to share in closing some data that will give you a sense of the magnitude of the challenge ahead and therefore demonstrate why we must come together now to elect the woman who breaks the link between leadership and maleness.

According to a recent report by the World Economic Forum, based on current trends, it will take exactly one hundred years to reach gender equality across 106 nations on measures including political empowerment, economic participation, health, and education. Covering the report for *Fast Company*, reporter Lydia Dishman added an important aside on the matter of *women's governmental power*: "The picture is even more bleak for women in politics, where we [the United States] are only 12% of the way to political equality (thanks to women's paltry representation in Congress and President Trump's cabinet)." At the current rate of women's election to the US Congress, it will take until after 2100 for the United States to reach congressional gender equality.

According to CAWP, 2018 may not be a "Year of the Woman" as far as *executive governmental office* is concerned:

- Only eight women are running for open US Senate seats and in just three states; the opportunity for women to run for the Senate is rare at a time when the Senate is a singular path to executive office.
- No incumbent women US senators are running for governor, and none as of this writing have announced a run for the presidency.
- Most of the women in gubernatorial races are running for open seats, and four of the six current women governors are up for reelection.

On the other hand, as previously mentioned, more women are running for governor than ever before in our nation's history. In the May 2018 Democratic House primaries, women candidates won in seventeen of the twenty races. Trends like these create a climate for change that can't be undervalued. This movement is motivated, big, and inspired. Women all over the country are hopeful and engaged.

"The least I can do is show and hold up everyone else who might want to come along or might be here. . . . if not me, who?" Maureen Martin, a candidate for county commission in Livingston County, Michigan, said in an inspiring video that accompanied a January 2018 *Time* magazine story. Characterizing the number of women like Martin who are running for office—of all kinds and everywhere—*Time* national correspondent Charlotte Alter wrote that this is "a grassroots movement that could change America. . . . Outside the Beltway, a transformation has already begun."

Transformational in intent, no doubt. But our movement needs a patriarchy-smashing focus if it is to matter forever, not just for another "Year of the Woman." We've had enough of those. It's time for a century of women. And then another. And another. I contend that the patriarchy-smashing focus we need is a wholehearted campaign to elect a woman president. Let's get started.

RESOURCES

"I CANNOT STOP FIGHTING."
—KÄTHE KOLLWITZ, GERMAN ARTIST, BERLIN, 1944

This section includes a selection of media that will inspire you to become a woman who elects Madam President and elects herself as a voice, an organizer, an ally, a writer, a public official, or a politically conscious artist. Every day there are more wonderful books, articles, movies, and TV shows you can add to this list. Search terms such as "feminism," "nasty woman," "woman power," or "women in politics," and you'll find them.

There are also increasingly more and more works of art by women who understand art's power to communicate sisterhood and women's equality. Deliberately, many of the resources listed here are books of and about women's art. My purpose in sharing them is to encourage you and your sisters to continue the inspirational, motivational work expressed in the Women's March posters that millions of women, maybe including you, created. Your posters keep us marching.

INSPIRING HISTORIES OF WOMEN POLITICAL LEADERS

Cleopatra: A Life by Stacy Schiff

Condoleezza Rice: A Memoir of My Extraordinary, Ordinary Family and Me by Condoleezza Rice

Crusade for Justice: The Autobiography of Ida B. Wells by Ida B. Wells

Dead Feminists: Historic Heroines in Living Color by Chandler O'Leary and Jessica Spring

Eleanor Roosevelt, Volume 1: The Early Years, 1884–1933; *Volume 2: The Defining Years, 1933–1938*; and *Volume 3: The War Years and After, 1939–1962* by Blanche Wiesen Cook

Fabulas Feminae by Susan Bee and Johanna Drucker

Fight Like a Girl: 50 Feminists Who Changed the World by Laura Barcella

Hidden Figures: The American Dream and the Untold Story of the Black Women Mathematicians Who Helped Win the Space Race by Margot Lee Shetterly

Lioness: Golda Meir and the Nation of Israel by Francine Klagsbrun

Make Trouble: Standing Up, Speaking Out, and Finding the Courage to Lead by Cecile Richards with Lauren Peterson

Mankiller: A Chief and Her People by Wilma Mankiller

My Beloved World by Sonia Sotomayor

Notorious RBG: The Life and Times of Ruth Bader Ginsburg by Irin Carmon and Shana Knizhnik

Sisters: The Lives of American Suffragists by Jean H. Baker

Sojourner Truth: A Life, A Symbol by Nell Irvin Painter

Twenty Years at Hull-House With Autobiographical Notes by Jane Addams

Unbought and Unbossed: Expanded Fortieth Anniversary Edition by Shirley Chisholm

The Woman Behind the New Deal: The Life and Legacy of Frances Perkins—Social Security, Unemployment Insurance, and the Minimum Wage by Kirstin Downey

Woman of Valor: Margaret Sanger and the Birth Control Movement in America by Ellen Chesler

For additional biographies and women's political books for all ages, see Teach a Girl to Lead (tag.rutgers.edu/books), a project of the Center for American Women and Politics.

HISTORIES AND ANALYSES OF AMERICAN WOMEN'S POLITICAL EXPERIENCE

All the Single Ladies: Unmarried Women and the Rise of an Independent Nation by Rebecca Traister

America's Women: 400 Years of Dolls, Drudges, Helpmates, and Heroines by Gail Collins

Backlash: The Undeclared War Against American Women by Susan Faludi

Breakthrough: The Making of America's First Woman President by Nancy L. Cohen

Broad Influence: How Women Are Changing the Way America Works by Jay Newton-Small

Chasing Hillary: Ten Years, Two Presidential Campaigns, and One Intact Glass Ceiling by Amy Chozick

The Destruction of Hillary Clinton: Untangling the Political Forces, Media Culture, and Assault on Fact That Decided the 2016 Election by Susan Bordo

Divided We Stand: The Battle Over Women's Rights and Family Values That Polarized American Politics by Marjorie J. Spruill

Feminism Is for Everybody: Passionate Politics by bell hooks

The Feminist Utopia Project: Fifty-Seven Visions of a Wildly Better Future edited by Alexandra Brodsky and Rachel Kauder Nalebuff

The H-Spot: The Feminist Pursuit of Happiness by Jill Filipovic

Men Explain Things to Me by Rebecca Solnit

The Mother of All Questions by Rebecca Solnit

Nasty Women: Feminism, Resistance, and Revolution in Trump's America edited by Samhita Mukhopadhyay and Kate Harding

Navigating Gendered Terrain: Stereotypes and Strategy in Political Campaigns by Kelly Dittmar

No More Nice Girls: Countercultural Essays by Ellen Willis

The Secret History of Wonder Woman by Jill Lepore

Sisters in Law: How Sandra Day O'Connor and Ruth Bader Ginsburg Went to the Supreme Court and Changed the World by Linda Hirshman

Thinking about the Presidency: The Primacy of Power by William G. Howell with David Milton Brent

Together We Rise: Behind the Scenes at the Protest Heard Around the World by the Women's March Organizers and Condé Nast

We Should All Be Feminists by Chimamanda Ngozi Adichie

We Were Feminists Once: From Riot Grrrl to CoverGirl®, the Buying and Selling of a Political Movement by Andi Zeisler

What Happened by Hillary Rodham Clinton

Why I March: Images from the Women's March Around the World by Abrams Image

Why We March: Signs of Protest and Hope—Voices from the Women's March by Artisan

The Witches: Suspicion, Betrayal, and Hysteria in 1692 Salem by Stacy Schiff

Women & Power: A Manifesto by Mary Beard

Also read my *HuffPost* opinion pieces at huffingtonpost.com/author/rebecca-672.

GUIDES TO RUNNING FOR OFFICE AND PUBLIC LEADERSHIP

"Campaign Tips from Cicero: The Art of Politics, from the Tiber to the Potomac" *Foreign Affairs* 91, no. 3 (May/June 2012) by Quintus Tullius Cicero and James Carville

Every Day Is Election Day: A Woman's Guide to Winning Any Office, from the PTA to the White House by Rebecca Sive

A Feminist Guide to the Resistance by *BUST* magazine

Organizing for Social Change: Midwest Academy Manual for Activists by Kim Bobo, Jackie Kendall, and Steve Max

Run for Something: A Real-Talk Guide to Fixing the System Yourself by Amanda Litman

Also read *Choke: What the Secrets of the Brain Reveal About Getting It Right When You Have To* by Sian Beilock.

Also visit the websites of organizations training and supporting women who want to run. These include:

- Artist Campaign School (artistcampaignschool.org)
- Center for American Women and Politics (cawp.rutgers.edu)
- Emerge America (emergeamerica.org)
- EMILY's List (emilyslist.org)
- Get Her Elected (getherelected.com)
- Higher Heights (higherheightsforamerica.org)
- IGNITE (ignitenational.org)
- New American Leaders (newamericanleaders.org)
- Run for Something (runforsomething.net)
- Running Start (runningstartonline.org)
- She Should Run (sheshouldrun.org)
- The United State of Women (theunitedstateofwomen.org)
- VoteRunLead (voterunlead.org)
- Women's Campaign School at Yale University (wcsyale.org)

BECOMING AN ACTIVIST

Indivisible: A Practical Guide for Resisting the Trump Agenda by Angel Padilla, Billy Fleming, Caroline Kavit, Emily Phelps, Ezra Levin, Gonzalo Martínez de Vedia, Indivar Dutta-Gupta, Jennay Ghowrwal, Jeremy Haile, Leah Greenberg, Mary Humphreys, Matt Traldi, Sara Clough, and Sarah Dohl, et al. (also available in Spanish)
Reveille for Radicals by Saul Alinsky
Rules for Radicals by Saul Alinsky

SCHOLARLY MONOGRAPHS ABOUT WOMEN IN POLITICS, LEADERSHIP, AND ACADEMICS

The Chisholm Effect: Black Women in American Politics 2018 by Higher Heights and the Center for American Women and Politics
Finding Gender in Election 2016: Lessons from Presidential Gender Watch by the Barbara Lee Family Foundation and the Center for American Women and Politics. (http://www.cawp.rutgers.edu/sites/default/files/resources/presidential-gender-gap_report_final.pdf)

Opportunity Knocks: Now Is the Time for Women Candidates by the Barbara Lee
Family Foundation

*Pipeline, Pathways, and Institutional Leadership: An Update on the Status of
Women in Higher Education* by Heather L. Johnson (on the related issue of
the low number of women in academic and research roles)

Many more helpful monographs are available at the websites of the Barbara Lee
Family Foundation (barbaraleefoundation.org) and the Center for American
Women and Politics (cawp.rutgers.edu).

INSPIRATIONAL BOOKS FOR YOUNG GIRLS THAT ARE GREAT FOR ADULT WOMEN, TOO

A Heart in Politics: Jeannette Rankin and Patsy T. Mink by Sue Davidson

A Is for Activist by Innosanto Nagara

Bad Girls Throughout History: 100 Remarkable Women Who Changed the World
by Ann Shen

Fearless Women: Courageous Females Who Refused to Be Denied (Real Lives
series) by Toby Reynolds and Paul Calver

Girls Think of Everything: Stories of Ingenious Inventions by Women by Catherine
Thimmesh and Melissa Sweet

Good Night Stories for Rebel Girls, Volumes 1 and 2 by Elena Favilli and Francesca
Cavallo

Grace for President by Kelly DiPucchio and LeUyen Pham

I Dissent: Ruth Bader Ginsburg Makes Her Mark by Debbie Levy and Elizabeth
Baddeley

If I Were President by Catherine Stier

Little Leaders: Bold Women in Black History by Vashti Harrison

Madam President by Lane Smith

*Madam President: The Extraordinary, True (and Evolving) Story of Women in
Politics* by Catherine Thimmesh and Douglas B. Jones

Patsy Mink by Stephanie Cham

*Rad American Women A-Z: Rebels, Trailblazers, and Visionaries Who Shaped Our
History . . . and Our Future!* by Kate Schatz and Miriam Klein Stahl

She Persisted: 13 American Women Who Changed the World by Chelsea Clinton
and Alexandra Boiger

*Side by Side/Lado a Lado: The Story of Dolores Huerta and Cesar Chavez/La
Historia de Dolores Huerta y Cesar Chavez* by Monica Brown and Joe Cepeda
Sonia Sotomayor: A Judge Grows in the Bronx/La Juez Que Crecio en el Bronx by
Jonah Winter and Edel Rodriguez
Women in Science: 50 Fearless Pioneers Who Changed the World by Rachel
Ignotofsky
Women Who Dared: 52 Stories of Fearless Daredevils, Adventurers, and Rebels by
Linda Skeers and Livi Gosling

See this article for more recent and forthcoming books: "Activism Anthologies
and Guides for Young Readers" by Natasha Gilmore, PublishersWeekly.com.

For a wonderful article about books of feminist folktales, see "These Feminist
Folktale Collections Belong In Every Young Girl's Bookshelf" by Crystal
Erickson, *Bust*.

FEMINIST MAGAZINES (PRINT AND ONLINE)

Bitch (bitchmedia.org)
BUST (bust.com)
Ms. Magazine (msmagazine.com)
Rebellious (rebelliousmagazine.com)
Wonkette (wonkette.com)

For more feminist magazines, see the list selected by the Feminist Majority
Foundation (feminist.org/research/zines.html), and visit Issuu.com, a web
platform where many are published, and search for "feminist magazines."

WOMEN WRITERS ON POLITICS AND GENDER ISSUES TO FOLLOW

I selected the women on the list below, in addition to those I've listed elsewhere, because I find their work in a variety of media and contexts helpful to understanding women's issues and politics in all of today's complexity.

Erin Burnett, *CNN* (cnn.com/profiles/erin-burnett-profile)
Irin Carmon, *Washington Post* (irincarmon.com)
Gail Collins, *New York Times* (nytimes.com/column/gail-collins)
Jill Filipovic, *New York Times* (nytimes.com/column/jill-filipovic)
Roxane Gay (roxanegay.com/writing/)
Michelle Goldberg, *New York Times* (nytimes.com/column/michelle-goldberg)
Linda Greenhouse, *New York Times* (nytimes.com/column/linda-greenhouse)
Nia-Malika Henderson, *CNN* (cnn.com/profiles/nia-malika-henderson)
Lily Herman (lilyherman.com)
Maria Hinojosa, NPR (npr.org/people/2100638/maria-hinojosa)
Margo Jefferson (heymancenter.org/people/margo-jefferson/)
Dahlia Lithwick, *Slate* (slate.com/authors.dahlia_lithwick.html)
Rachel Maddow, MSNBC (msnbc.com/maddowblog)
Amanda Marcotte, *Salon* (salon.com/writer/amanda_marcotte)
Jay Newton-Small, *Time* (time.com/author/jay-newton-small)
Soledad O'Brien (starfishmediagroup.com/soledad2/)
Katha Pollitt, *Nation* (thenation.com/authors/katha-pollitt/)
Ai-jen Poo (domesticworkers.org/ai-jen-poo)
Joy-Ann Reid, MSNBC (msnbc.com/am-joy/joy-reid-biography)
Jennifer Rubin, *Washington Post,* (washingtonpost.com/people/jennifer-rubin/)
Julie Scelfo, *New York Times* (nytimes.com/by/julie-scelfo)
Marianne Schnall (marianneschnall.com/)
Debbie Stoller and Laurie Henzel, *BUST* magazine (bust.com)
Amanda Terkel, *HuffPost* (huffingtonpost.com/author/amanda-terkel)
Rebecca Traister, *New York Magazine* (nymag.com/author/rebecca traister)
Karen Tumulty, *Washington Post* (washingtonpost.com/people/karen-tumulty)
Jessica Valenti, *Guardian* (theguardian.com/profile/jessicavalenti)
Andi Zeisler, *Bitch Media* (bitchmedia.org/profile/andi-zeisler)

SOME MOVIES ABOUT STRONG WOMEN AND GIRLS WHO INSPIRE KINDNESS AND ACTION FOR GOOD

American Hustle
Bend It Like Beckham
The Blind Side
Election
Elizabeth
Erin Brockovich

Fargo
The Help
Hidden Figures
Joy
Legally Blonde

Legally Blonde 2: Red,
    White & Blonde
Little Miss Sunshine
Monster's Ball
Pitch Perfect
Precious

COMEDIES ABOUT WOMEN WHO SUPPORT EACH OTHER

Bridesmaids
Clueless
Divine Secrets of the
    Ya-Ya Sisterhood

Girls Trip
The Heat
A League of Their Own

Romy and Michele's
    High School Reunion

INSTRUCTIVE TV SHOWS ABOUT WOMEN WHO LEAD IN VARIOUS WAYS

The Americans
BrainDead
The Crown

Friday Night Lights
Game of Thrones
The Good Wife

House of Cards
Prime Suspect
The West Wing

PODCASTS ABOUT WOMEN AND POLITICS

Backtalk and Popaganda by Bitch Media (bitchmedia.org/feminist-podcasts)
Two Broads Talking Politics (stitcher.com/podcast/two-broads-talking-politics)

For additional podcasts to follow, see the following lists compiled by Estelle Tang for *Elle* (elle.com/culture/career-politics/g30167/best-political-podcasts/) and by Nisha Chittal for Medium (medium.com/@nishachittal/8-great-women-centric-podcasts-to-listen-to-in-2017-c0960cb356cb).

FEMINIST CRAFT BOOKS

Crafting the Resistance: 35 Projects for Craftivists, Protestors, and Women Who Persist by Heather Marano and Lara Neel

Crafting With Feminism: 25 Girl-Powered Projects to Smash the Patriarchy by Bonnie Burton

The Feminist Activity Book by Gemma Correll

Feminist Icon Cross-Stitch: 30 Daring Designs to Celebrate Strong Women by Anna Fleiss and Lauren Mancuso

Protest Knits: Got Needles? Get Knitting! by Geraldine Warner

Really Cross Stitch: For When You Just Want to Stab Something a Lot by Rayna Fahey

Subversive Cross Stitch: 50 F*cking Clever Designs for Your Sassy Side by Julie Jackson

Visit Shannon Downey's Badass Cross Stitch (badasscrossstitch.com) and the website Craftivism.com (craftivism.com/manifesto) for inspiration and information about "craftivism," where "your craft is your voice."

FEMINIST COLORING BOOKS

Avie's Dreams: An Afro-Feminist Coloring Book by Makeda Lewis

The Badass Feminist Coloring Book (Volume 1) by Ijeoma Oluo

Beyoncé: The Queen Bey Coloring Book by Sophia Lorraine

Boss Babes: A Coloring and Activity Book for Grown-Ups by Michelle Volansky

The Future Is Female: Feminist Adult Coloring Book by Creative Collective Design

The Post-Structuralist Vulva Coloring Book by Elly Blue and Meggyn Pomerleau

Rad American Women Coloring Book by Individuality Books

The Ruth Bader Ginsburg Coloring Book: A Tribute to the Always Colorful and Often Inspiring Life of the Supreme Court Justice Known as RBG by Tom F. O'Leary

There are also many coloring books featuring Hillary Clinton, both by those who like her and by those who really don't.

COMIC BOOKS, CARTOONS, AND GRRRL ZINES BY WOMEN AUTHORS AND ARTISTS

Awkward and Definition: The High School Comic Chronicles of Ariel Schrag; *Potential: The High School Comic Chronicles of Ariel Schrag*; and *Likewise: The High School Comic Chronicles of Ariel Schrag*, a series by Ariel Schrag, the author of the 2014 novel *Adam*

Bitch Planet, Vol. 1: Extraordinary Machine by Kelly Sue DeConnick and Valentine De Landro

Dykes to Watch Out For by Alison Bechdel; go to http://dykestowatchoutfor.com for Bechdel's other books and blog

Juicy Mother: Celebration and *Juicy Mother 2: How They Met* edited by Jennifer Camper

The Good Times Are Killing Me; *One! Hundred! Demons!*; *What It Is*; *Cruddy: An Illustrated Novel*; and *The! Greatest! of! Marlys!* by Lynda Barry

See also the works of Annie Nocenti, comic book author, journalist, writer, and filmmaker (annienocenti.com). Other cartoonists of note include Nicole Hollander, who, since publishing *That Woman Must Be On Drugs* in 1981, has continued to spoof gender stereotypes and women's lives, and Ann Telnaes, an editorial cartoonist for the *Washington Post* (washingtonpost.com/people/ann-telnaes). For independently published feminist thinking, see the Grrrl Zine Network (grrrlzines.net/about.htm).

ANTHOLOGIES OF COMICS

Comics for Choice: Illustrated Abortion Stories, History, and Politics edited by Hazel Newlevant and Whit Taylor

The Complete Wimmen's Comix by Trina Robbins, Gary Groth, Aline Kominsky-Crumb, and Diane Noomin

No Straight Lines: Four Decades of Queer Comics edited by Justin Hall

RESIST! Volumes 1 and 2 by Françoise Mouly and Nadja Spiegelman

The Riot Grrrl Collection edited by Lisa Darms, featuring an essay by Johanna Fateman

Stuck in the Middle: 17 Comics from an Unpleasant Age edited by Ariel Schrag

Explore others at:

AV Club (aux.avclub.com/10-female-cartoonists-
you-need-to-know-1798259254 and aux.avclub.
com/10-great-cartoonists-you-need-to-know-celebrating-inte-1798244929)
Hyperallergic (hyperallergic.com/114326/
pretty-in-ink-women-cartoonists-in-the-history-of-comics/)
Bleeding Cool (bleedingcool.com/2017/05/04/
british-women-cartoonist-comic-artists-exhibition-london-kicks-off/)

STUDIES OF FEMINIST GRAPHIC ARTS AND PUBLISHING

Girls to the Front: The True Story of the Riot Grrrl Revolution by Sara Marcus
Girl Zines: Making Media, Doing Feminism by Alison Piepmeier and Andi Zeisler
Graphic Details: Jewish Women's Confessional Comics in Essays and Interviews
edited by Sarah Lightman

WRITINGS ABOUT WOMEN'S FINE ART, TRADITIONAL WOMEN'S CRAFTS, FEMINISM, AND POLITICS

"Artists Behind the 'She Inspires' Exhibit Empower Women to Make a Political
Statement," by Elizabeth Strassner, *Bustle*, May 3, 2017 (bustle.com/p/
artists-behind-the-she-inspires-exhibit-empower-women-to-make-a-
political-statement-55282)
"Chicago Women's Graphics Collective," Chicago Women's Liberation Union
Herstory Project website (cwluherstory.org/chicago-womens-graphics
-collective-1/)
The Dinner Party: A Symbol of Our Heritage and *Through the Flower: My Struggle
as a Woman Artist* by Judy Chicago
"Feminism & Feminist Art," *Art History Archive* (arthistoryarchive.com/
arthistory/feminist/)
Fray: Art and Textile Politics by Julia Bryan-Wilson
From the Center: Feminist Essays on Women's Art by Lucy R. Lippard
The Guerrilla Girls' Bedside Companion to the History of Western Art and *Bitches,
Bimbos, and Ballbreakers: The Guerrilla Girls' Illustrated Guide to Female
Stereotypes* by the Guerrilla Girls

"Herstory: Feminist Theory and Resistance in Art & Cinema," *University of California Press Blog*, January 19, 2018 (ucpress.edu/blog/34399/herstory-feminist-theory-in-art-cinema/)

"How and Why Did the Guerrilla Girls Alter the Art World Establishment in New York City, 1985–1995?" by Suzanne Lustig under the direction of Kathryn Kish Sklar, *Women and Social Movements in the United States, 1600–2000*, Spring 2002 (womhist.alexanderstreet.com/ggirls/intro.htm)

"Judy Chicago, the Godmother," by Sasha Weiss, *T: The New York Times Style Magazine*, February 7, 2018

"Nasty Women Around the World," *Nasty Women Exhibitions* (nastywomenexhibition.org/other-nasty-venues/)

"Popular Feminist Art Books," *Goodreads* (goodreads.com/shelf/show/feminist-art)

"Protest Art, and Institutional Support of It, Is More Vital Than Ever," by Jon Kessler, *Hyperallergic*, September 26, 2017 (hyperallergic.com/402219/protest-art-and-institutional-support-of-it-is-more-vital-than-ever/)

Rad Women Worldwide: Artists and Athletes, Pirates and Punks, and Other Revolutionaries Who Shaped History by Kate Schatz and Miriam Klein Stahl

Radical Decadence: Excess in Contemporary Feminist Textiles and Craft by Julia Skelly

The Reckoning: Women Artists of the New Millennium by Eleanor Heartney, Helaine Posner, Nancy Princenthal, and Sue Scott

See Red Women's Workshop: Feminist Posters 1974–1990 by Prudence Stevenson, Susan Mackie, Anne Robinson, and Jess Baines

The Subversive Stitch: Embroidery and the Making of the Feminine by Rozsika Parker

WACK!: Art and the Feminist Revolution edited by Cornelia Butler and Lisa Gabrielle Mark

We Wanted a Revolution: Black Radical Women 1965–85: A Sourcebook edited by Catherine Morris and Rujeko Hockley

"What Makes Contemporary Art Feminist? An Art Genome Project Case Study," by Ellen Yoshi Tani, *Artsy for Education*, January 16, 2015 (artsy.net/article/theartgenomeproject-what-makes-contemporary-art-feminist-an-art)

Women × Women, presented by Absolut Art & Tictail (tictail.com/absolutart)

"Why Have There Been No Great Women Artists?" by Linda Nochlin; also see the article *"An Illustrated Guide to Linda Nochlin's 'Why Have There Been No Great Women Artists?"* by Tiernan Morgan and Lauren Purje, *Hyperallergic*, May 23, 2017

Women, Art, and Power and Other Essays by Linda Nochlin
Women Artists: The Linda Nochlin Reader edited by Maura Reilly

See *Artbook* (artbook.com/feminist-art.html) for a list of monographs about individual women artists. Also see *Reclaiming the Body: Feminist Art in America* (michaelblackwoodproductions.com/old/arts_reclaimingbody.php), a documentary featuring Linda Nochlin and other experts on women's art and feminism.

ENDNOTES

INTRODUCTION: "GIRLS CAN BE ANYTHING, JUST NOT PRESIDENT"

2 **"It has to be taken":** Lisa Madigan (Illinois attorney general), interview by the author, February 2018.

2 **whether legislative or executive:** Saskia Brechenmacher, "Tackling Women's Underrepresentation in US Politics: Comparative Perspectives from Europe," *Carnegie Endowment for International Peace*, February 20, 2018.

2 **that benefit women and girls:** Swanee Hunt and Andrea Dew Steele, "A Seismic Shift in Government Is Coming, and Here's Who Will Drive It," *CNN*, April 21, 2018.

2 **wanted to vote her in then:** Gregory Krieg, "It's Official: Clinton Swamps Trump in Popular Vote," *CNN*, December 22, 2016.

2 **"protest in US history":** Ai-jen Poo, "A Woman's Work Is Never Done (in a Democracy)," in *Together We Rise: Behind the Scenes at the Protest Heard Around the World* (New York: Dey Street Books, 2018): 94.

3 **where most women are elected:** "Women in Elective Office 2018," Center for American Women and Politics.

4 **"leadership is synonymous with maleness":** Bennett, "Girls Can Be Anything."

4 **run for office can win:** Rebecca Sive, *Every Day Is Election Day: A Woman's Guide to Winning Any Office, from the PTA to the White House* (Chicago: Chicago Review Press, 2013).

5 **"I want it to happen in my lifetime":** Madigan interview, February 2018.

7 **work across party lines to do so:** Sheryl Gay Stolberg, "Proof That Women Are the Better Dealmakers in the Senate," *New York Times*, February 19, 2015.

PART ONE: WE'RE STILL HERE

10 **State's Attorney Foxx put it:** Kimberly M. Foxx (Cook County, Illinois, state's attorney), interview by the author, February 2018.

11 **"you really can do everything":** Madigan interview, February 2018.

11 **According to State's Attorney Foxx:** Foxx interview, February 2018.

11 **"the eyes of being a woman":** Foxx interview, February 2018.

11 **Clinton won the popular vote:** Krieg, "It's Official: Clinton Swamps Trump in Popular Vote."

11 **"candidate in any other election":** Clare Foran, "Women Aren't Responsible for Hillary Clinton's Defeat," *Atlantic*, November 13, 2016.

14 **"19 in Wisconsin and Minnesota":** Ronald Brownstein, "White Women in the Rustbelt Are Turning on Trump," *Atlantic*, February 8, 2018.

14 **run for office in historic numbers:** Heather Caygle, "Record-Breaking Number of Women Run for Office," *Politico*, March 8, 2018.

16 **the mayors are women:** "Women Mayors in US Cities 2018," Center for American Women and Politics.

16 **(all but three since 1975):** Marie Solis, "A Record Number of Women Are Running for Governor in 2018," *Newsweek*, January 2, 2018.

16 **28.5 percent in 2000:** "Historical Summary of Women in Statewide Elective Executive Office: 1969–Current," Center for American Women and Politics.

16 **seven of fifty state attorneys general:** "Women in Statewide Elective Executive Office 2018," Center for American Women and Politics.

16 **"both donors and the news media":** Jonathan Martin, "Democrats Mount Effort to Recruit Women as State Attorneys General," *New York Times*, September 19, 2017.

16 **appointed to fill her husband's seat:** "Milestones for Women in American Politics," Center for American Women and Politics.

17 **"was a man":** Nancy L. Cohen, *Breakthrough: The Making of America's First Woman President* (Berkeley, CA: Counterpoint, 2016), 258.

17 **appointed in 1997:** Rich Miller, "Leader Currie to Retire at End of Term," *Capitol Fax*, September 15, 2017.

17 **the only woman serving on the court:** Adam Liptak, "On Tour With Notorious RBG, Judicial Rock Star," *New York Times*, February 8, 2018.

17 **follow for another twenty years:** "Milestones for Women in American Politics." Center for American Women and Politics.

CHAPTER I: WE HOLD THESE TRUTHS TO BE SELF-EVIDENT

20 **"right to vote in 1870":** Annette Gordon-Reed, "Female Trouble," *New York Review of Books*, February 8, 2018.

21 **"political and situational factors":** Claire Cain Miller, "Women Actually Do Govern Differently," *New York Times*, November 10, 2016.

21 BUT CAN SHE TYPE?: "But Can She Type? [Golda Meir]," Library of Congress, ca. 1970.

21 **"be put under curfew":** Letty Cottin Pogrebin, "Golda Meir," *Jewish Women: A Comprehensive Historical Encyclopedia*, March 20, 2009, Jewish Women's Archive.

22 **than their male counterparts:** Lindsey Cormack, "Gender and Vote Revelation Strategy in the United States Congress," *Journal of Gender Studies* 25, no. 6 (Summer 2015): 626–640.

22 **sexual assault in congressional offices:** Joe Williams, "All 22 Female Senators Demand Leadership Acts on Sexual Harassment Legislation," *Roll Call*, March 28, 2018.

22 **to carry out the affair:** Richard Fausset and Mitch Smith, "Megan Barry, Nashville Mayor, Pleads Guilty to Theft and Agrees to Resign," *New York Times*, March 6, 2018.

22 **"for all our signs in Nashville":** Susanna Rustin, "Can Cities Be Feminist? Inside the Global Rise of Female Mayors," *Guardian*, October 12, 2016.

23 **"not just roads and rail":** Rustin, "Can Cities Be Feminist?"

23 **on the floor of the US Senate:** Marie Solis, "Tammy Duckworth May Have to Breastfeed in a Bathroom Off the Senate Floor, Says Former Senate Parliamentarian," *Newsweek*, February 15, 2018.

23 **was passed in April 2018:** Sheryl Gay Stolberg, "'It's About Time': A Baby Comes to the Senate Floor," *New York Times*, April 19, 2018.

23 **"never make it to a vote":** Miller, "Women Actually Do Govern Differently."

CHAPTER 2: COULD BE ASLEEP, FORCED ME TO PROTEST

26 **"all politics are local politics":** Amber Frost, "Bring Back the Feminists of WITCH (Women's International Terrorist Conspiracy from Hell)!" *Dangerous Minds*, February 6, 2015.

26 **"To burn CTA in freedoms' fire":** Frost, "Bring Back the Feminists of WITCH."

28 **"rigged towards Wellesley girls":** Frost, "Bring Back the Feminists of WITCH."

28 **"stubborn with a turbulent reputation":** Marilynne K. Roach, "9 Reasons You Might Have Been Suspected of Witchcraft in 1692," *HuffPost*, October 2, 2013.

28 **deep and compelling detail:** Stacy Schiff, *The Witches: Suspicion, Betrayal, and Hysteria in 1692 Salem* (New York: Back Bay Books, 2015).

28 **"the worst misogynist atrocity in American history":** Megan O'Grady, "*Vogue*'s Fall Books Guide: The Best Books of the Season," *Vogue*, September 9, 2015.

29 **"resurgence of occultism among millennials":** Michelle Goldberg, "Season of the Witch," *New York Times*, November 3, 2017.

29 **"arbiter of your own justice":** Goldberg, "Season of the Witch."

CHAPTER 3: THEY TRIED TO BURY US. THEY DIDN'T KNOW WE WERE SEEDS

32 **who wouldn't be buried:** Jessica H., "They Tried to Bury Us. They Didn't Know We Were Seeds," *J.H. Fearless* (blog), November 24, 2014.

32 **at age forty-eight:** "Chisholm, Shirley Anita," US House of Representatives History, Art & Archives, accessed April 1, 2018.

32 **"unbought and unbossed":** "Chisholm, Shirley Anita," US House of Representatives History, Art & Archives.

32 **"This 'woman thing' is so deep":** Karen Foerstel and Herbert N. Foerstel, *Climbing the Hill: Gender Conflict in Congress*, (Westport, CT: Praeger, 1996), 30.

34 **"more veterans in my district than trees":** "Chisholm, Shirley Anita," US House of Representatives History, Art & Archives.

35 **low-income mothers and children:** Dovid Zaklikowski, "Turning Disappointment into Food for the Hungry," TheRebbe.org, accessed April 1, 2018.

35 **women of color among them:** "People Search: Women in Congress, 91st (1969–1971)," US House of Representatives History, Art & Archives, accessed April 1, 2018.

35 **half were African American:** Jo Freeman, "Shirley Chisholm's 1972 Presidential Campaign," University of Illinois at Chicago Women's Political History Project, February 2005, archived from the original on November 11, 2014.

35 **"Men are men":** James Barron, "Shirley Chisholm, 'Unbossed' Pioneer in Congress, Is Dead at 80," *New York Times*, January 3, 2005.

CHAPTER 4: THIS PUSSY GRABS BACK

37 **"You can do anything":** "Transcript: Donald Trump's Taped Comments about Women," *New York Times*, October 8, 2016.

37 **"locker room banter":** Allan Smith, "Melania Trump Responds: 'Unacceptable and Offensive to Me,'" *Business Insider*, October 8, 2016.

38 **on Chicago's Near West Side:** Jane Addams Hull-House Museum website, accessed April 1, 2018.

38 **member of a presidential cabinet:** Leah W. Sprague, "Her Life: The Woman Behind the New Deal," Frances Perkins Center, June 1, 2014.

38 **the nickname stuck:** Anne Firor Scott, "Saint Jane and the Ward Boss," *American Heritage* 12, no. 1 (December 1960).

39 **"merging with the water line":** Scott, "Saint Jane and the Ward Boss."

40 **"constituents must be permanent'":** Scott, "Saint Jane and the Ward Boss."

40 *were even granted property rights:* Bruce D. Janu and Wendy Hamand Venet, "Mary Livermore and the Illinois Women's Suffrage Movement," Illinois Periodicals Online, accessed January 16, 2018.

40 **born a slave in 1862:** "Ida B. Wells Biography," Biography.com, accessed January 16, 2018.

40 **legislature for many years:** Louis Menand, *The Metaphysical Club: A Story of Ideas in America,* (New York: Farrar, Straus and Giroux, 2001) 306–307.

40 **which Wells attended:** "Ida B. Wells Biography," Biography.com.

40 **ultimately losing the case:** "Ida B. Wells Biography," Biography.com.

41 **"three of our best young men":** "Ida B. Wells, 'Lynch Law in All Its Phases,'" Voices of Democracy: The US Oratory Project, transcribed from speech on February 13, 1893.

41 **she would be killed:** "Ida B. Wells Biography," Biography.com.

41 **"as if they were brutes":** Ida B. Wells, "Lynch Law in All Its Phases," Voice of Democracy.

41 **focus of "black women's clubs":** "African American Reformers: The Club Movement," National Women's History Museum.

41 **its board of directors:** "Oldest and Boldest," National Association for the Advancement of Colored People.

42 **only Wells actually ran:** "Ida B. Wells Biography," Biography.com.

42 **garbage inspector for her ward:** "Jane Addams – Biographical," Nobelprize.org, from *Nobel Lectures, Peace 1926–1950,* editor Frederick W. Haberman (Amsterdam: Elsevier Publishing Company, 1972).

42 **"really know what is wrong":** Jane Addams, *Twenty Years at Hull-House With Autobiographical Notes* (New York: New American Library, Third Printing, 1961), 70.

43 **"back what I have said":** Ida B. Wells and Alfreda M. Duster, ed. *Crusade for Justice: The Autobiography of Ida B. Wells* (Chicago: University of Chicago Press, 1970), 64, 370.

CHAPTER 5: THE PATRIARCHY AIN'T GONNA SMASH ITSELF

45 **"the world is structurally engineered against women":** Susan Faludi, "The Patriarchs Are Falling. The Patriarchy Is Stronger Than Ever," *New York Times,* December 28, 2017.

46 **institutions that run their lives:** Mary Beard, *Women & Power: A Manifesto* (New York: Liveright Publishing Corporation, 2017).

46 **diversity and inclusion statements galore:** Joanne Lipman, "How Diversity Training Infuriates Men and Fails Women," *Time,* January 25, 2018.

46 **embedded in modern American institutions:** Kim Parker, Juliana Menasce Horowitz, Wendy Wang, Anna Brown, and Eileen Patten, "Chapter 3: Obstacles to Female Leadership," *Women and Leadership: Public Says Women Are Equally Qualified, but Barriers Persist,* Pew Research Center, January 14, 2015.

46 **fewer women achieving executive leadership roles:** Parker et al., "Chapter 3: Obstacles to Female Leadership."

46 **women CEOs in the Fortune 500:** Claire Cain Miller, "The Number of Female Chief Executives Is Falling," *New York Times,* May 23, 2018.

46 **Center for American Progress (CAP):** Judith Warner and Danielle Corley, "The Women's Leadership Gap," Center for American Progress, May 21, 2017.

47 **"Than Men Named John":** Justin Wolfers, "Fewer Women Run Big Companies Than Men Named John," *New York Times*, March 2, 2015.

47 **"key leadership roles in the United States":** Warner and Corley, "The Women's Leadership Gap."

48 **"the place where the buck stops":** Karen Tumulty, "'If We Don't Run, Then We Won't Achieve.' Why a Record Number of Women Are Eyeing a Run for Governor," *Washington Post*, January 1, 2018.

48 **nomination for governor in Georgia:** Jonathan Martin and Alexander Burns, "Stacey Abrams Wins Georgia Democratic Primary for Governor, Making History," *New York Times*, May 22, 2018.

48 **governor in New Mexico:** Kelly Dittmar, "After #SuperTuesday Primaries, Women Candidates on Path to Make History in Multiple States," Gender Watch 2018, June 6, 2018.

48 **"running for governor this year":** Jonathan Martin and Alexander Burns, "Democratic Women Are Running for Governor. Men and Money Stand in Their Way." *New York Times*, June 11, 2018.

48 **the governor of a state:** David J. Andersen and John Weingart, "Governors Who Became President," Rutgers University Eagleton Institute of Politics Center on the American Governor, 2014.

48 **were governors:** Andersen and Weingart, "Governors Who Became President."

49 **"more political agency than in the past":** Lauren Holter, "Governor Races in 2018 Could See More Women Running Than Ever Before," *Bustle*, January 2, 2018.

49 **"It's just how I'm wired":** Tumulty, "'If We Don't Run, Then We Won't Achieve.'"

CHAPTER 6: WE'RE NOT BILLIONAIRE WHITE MEN

51 **exacerbated by race discrimination:** Eileen Patten, "Racial, Gender Wage Gaps Persist in US Despite Some Progress," Pew Research Center, July 1, 2016.

51 **47 percent of our country's workforce:** Mark DeWolf, "12 Stats about Working Women," US Department of Labor blog, March 1, 2017.

51 **fewer opportunities for advancement:** Patten, "Racial, Gender Wage Gaps Persist in US."

51 **at least three-fourths of the workforce:** DeWolf, "12 Stats about Working Women."

52 **Institute for Women's Policy Research:** Elyse Shaw, Ariane Hegewisch, Emma Williams-Baron, and Barbara Gault, *Undervalued and Underpaid in America: Women in Low-Wage, Female-Dominated Jobs*, Institute for Women's Policy Research, November 17, 2016.

52 **"will be called to fill those roles":** Claire Landsbaum, "Most Low-Wage Workers in the United States Are Women, Study Finds," *The Cut*, December 28, 2016.

52 **mothers with children under 18:** DeWolf, "12 Stats about Working Women."

52 **headed by a single mother:** US Census Bureau, "The Majority of Children Live With Two Parents, Census Bureau Reports," press release, November 17, 2016.

53 **seemingly with increasing frequency:** Kristen Bialik, "Americans Deepest in Poverty Lost More Ground in 2016," Pew Research Center, October 6, 2017.

53 **time raising money:** Tim Roemer, "Why Do Congressmen Spend Only Half Their Time Serving Us?" *Newsweek*, July 29, 2015.

54 **only eleven were black:** Mfonobong Nsehe, "The Black Billionaires 2018," *Forbes*, March 7, 2018.

54 **upper ranks of big companies:** Warner and Corley, "The Women's Leadership Gap."

54 **and 256 were women:** Jennifer Wang, "The Richest Women in the World 2018," *Forbes*, March 6, 2018.

54 **want to run for office:** EMILY's List, "Over 34,000 Women Want to Run for Office," press release, February 27, 2018.

CHAPTER 7: BUILD BRIDGES, NOT WALLS

57 **Black Power Movement:** Lakisha Odlum, "The Black Power Movement," Digital Public Library of America, 2015.

57 **"the new pluralism":** Irving M. Levine, *The New Pluralism* (National Project on Ethnic America).

58 **"as transcendent common interests":** Bertram H. Gold, "Who Speaks for the Jews," text of address by Gold, executive vice president of the American Jewish Committee, at the committee's annual meeting, New York City, May 4, 1972, cited in Arthur A. Goren, *The Politics and Public Culture of American Jews* (Bloomington: Indiana University Press, 1999), 262.

58 ***Guía para las Mujeres de Chicago:*** Inforwomen, *Chicago Women's Directory / Guía para las Mujeres de Chicago* (Chicago, 1974).

59 **"social justice for all Americans":** Nancy Seifer, *Absent from the Majority: Working Class Women in America*, Middle America pamphlet series (National Project on Ethnic America, 1973).

59 IT'S ABOUT BASIC HUMAN DECENCY: White House Office of the First Lady, "Transcript: Michelle Obama's Speech on Donald Trump's Alleged Treatment of Women," NPR, October 13, 2016.

59 **they chose Donald Trump:** Aamna Mohdin, "American Women Voted Overwhelmingly for Clinton, Except the White Ones," *Quartz*, November 9, 2016.

59 **American women Seifer wrote about:** "Historic Gender Gap Isn't Enough to Propel Clinton to Victory in 2016 Presidential Race," Center for American Women and Politics, November 9, 2016.

59 ***The Hidden Injuries of Class:*** Richard Sennett and Jonathan Cobb, *The Hidden Injuries of Class* (New York: Alfred A. Knopf, 1972).

60 **sexual harassment in congressional offices:** Williams, "All 22 Female Senators."

60 **"support their own families":** Seifer, *Absent from the Majority.*

61 **"ruined landscape of toxic waste":** Robert Kuttner, "Hidden Injuries of Class, Race, and Culture," *American Prospect*, October 3, 2016.

CHAPTER 8: DEAR TRUMP: YOU GOT 99 PROBLEMS AND THIS BITCH IS I

64 **"tend to turn against her":** Anna North, "Hillary Clinton Has a Theory about Why She Lost With White Women," *Vox*, September 12, 2017.

64 **so be it:** "Madonna," *People* archive, July 27, 1992.

64 **"behind being a 'bitch'":** MTV, "Nicki Minaj: 'My Time Now,'" MTV Music Specials, 2010.

64 **According to CAWP:** "Gender Differences in Voter Turnout," Center for American Women and Politics, July 20, 2017.

65 **the silent generation:** Richard Fry, "Millennials Projected to Overtake Baby Boomers as America's Largest Generation," Pew Research Center, March 1, 2018.

65 **"capacity to effect change":** Maya Kosoff, "Can Millennial Women Decide the Next Election?" *Vanity Fair*, February 27, 2018.

66 **support activist campaigns:** Kosoff, "Can Millennial Women Decide the Next Election?"

66 **contributing editor Bill Scher:** Bill Scher, "Why 2020 Will Be the Year of the Woman," *Politico Magazine*, November 24, 2017.

66 **"the woman's hour must again strike":** Scher, "Why 2020 Will Be the Year of the Woman."

66 **"the inevitable misogynistic attacks":** Scher, "Why 2020 Will Be the Year of the Woman."

CHAPTER 9: HEAR US HOLLER

69 ***Who Refused to Be Denied:*** Toby Reynolds and Paul Calver, *Fearless Women: Courageous Females Who Refused to Be Denied*, Real Lives series (Hauppauge, NY: Barron's Educational Series, 2017).

70 **other rock-and-roll stars:** "Sister Rosetta Tharpe," Rock & Roll Hall of Fame, 2018.

70 ***Who Changed the World:*** Chelsea Clinton, *She Persisted: 13 American Women Who Changed the World* (New York: Philomel Books, 2017).

70 **"Nevertheless, she persisted":** Amy B. Wang, "'Nevertheless, She Persisted' Becomes New Battle Cry After McConnell Silences Elizabeth Warren," *Washington Post*, February 8, 2017.

72 **"with a vengeance":** James Hill, "West Side Inspiration Nancy Jefferson, 69," *Chicago Tribune*, October 19, 1992.

72 **"overcome on the campaign trail":** Kelly Dittmar, "A Different Measure of Success for Women Running in 2018," Gender Watch 2018, March 28, 2018.

CHAPTER 10: BEYONCÉ RUNS THE WORLD

75 **"(who run this motha', yeah)":** Beyoncé, "Run the World (Girls)," *4*, Columbia Records, 2011, compact disc.

76 **repeated four times:** Beyoncé, "Run the World (Girls)."

76 **"'cause I slay":** Beyoncé, "Formation," *Lemonade*, Columbia Records, 2016, compact disc.

77 **"adding spice to her meals":** Kevin Doyle, "Hillary Clinton Rarely Listens to Her iPod, Always Packs Tabasco Sauce," *Condé Nast Traveler*, August 30, 2012.

77 **for Clinton to win:** Mohdin, "American Women Voted Overwhelmingly."

78 **"To say and do whatever I please":** Lesley Gore, "You Don't Own Me," Mercury Records, 1963, seven-inch single.

79 **"But lead me all around":** Andrews, Inez, vocalist, "Lord Don't Move the Mountain" by Doris Akers, *Lord Don't Move the Mountain*. Jewel Records, 1995. Compact disc.

CHAPTER 11: FLAG DAY

82 **United States entered the war:** Krishnadev Calamur, "A Short History of 'America First,'" *Atlantic*, January 21, 2017.

84 **"majority still do not":** Calamur, "A Short History of 'America First.'"

84 **in World War II:** Francis X. Clines, "Trump Quits Grand Old Party for New," *New York Times*, October 25, 1999.

84 **"be only, 'America First'":** John Fritze and Alison Knezevich, "President Trump: 'From This Day Forward It's Only Going to Be America First,'" *Baltimore Sun*, January 20, 2017.

CHAPTER 12: HISTORY HAS ITS EYES ON ALL OF US

88 **never been a woman president:** "Women in Elective Office 2018," Center for American Women and Politics.

88 **5 percent of US Congress:** "Women in Elective Office 2018," Center for American Women and Politics.

88 **served in the US Senate:** "History of Women in the US Congress," Center for American Women and Politics, last updated 2018.

88 **book on women's advancement:** Sheryl Sandberg, *Lean In: Women, Work, and the Will to Lead* (New York: Alfred A. Knopf, 2013).

90 **the assembly line instead:** Marcia Walker, "Wyatt, Rev. Addie (1924–2012)," BlackPast.org.

90 **United Packinghouse Workers of America:** "Black History Month: Addie Wyatt," United Food and Commercial Workers Union Local 324, February 15, 2018.

90 **Montgomery, Alabama, in 1965:** "International Civil Rights Walk of Fame: Addie L. Wyatt," National Park Service, accessed January 9, 2018.

90 **Southern Christian Leadership Conference (SCLC):** "Addie Wyatt: UFCW Lighthouse," United Food and Commercial Workers Union Local 324, April 9, 1952.

90 **civil rights in the South:** "Southern Christian Leadership Conference (SCLC)," The Martin Luther King, Jr. Research and Education Institute at Stanford University, January 10, 1957.

90 **lives of African Americans**: Walker, "Wyatt, Rev. Addie (1924–2012)."

90 **Scala's *Chicago Tribune* obituary:** Emma Graves Fitzsimmons, "Florence Scala, 1918–2007," *Chicago Tribune*, August 29, 2007.

91 **"live in a real democracy":** Fitzsimmons, "Florence Scala, 1918–2007."

PART TWO: I AM DONE BEING QUIET

93 *the Women's Liberation Movement:* Robin Morgan, ed., *Sisterhood Is Powerful: An Anthology of Writings from the Women's Liberation Movement* (New York: Random House, 1970).

95 **well-paid men:** Joanna Rothkopf, "An Investigation: Which Presidential Campaigns Have the Largest Gender Wage Disparities?" *Jezebel,* March 15, 2016.

96 **"No more nice girls":** Ellen Willis, *No More Nice Girls: Countercultural Essays* (Hanover, NH: University Press of New England for Wesleyan University Press, 1992).

97 **and the American Revolution:** "Thomas Paine Biography," Biography.com, accessed June 6, 2018.

97 **"a whore of my soul":** Saul Alinsky, *Reveille for Radicals* (New York: Vintage Books, 1969).

97 **"hate conditions, not individuals":** Alinsky, *Reveille for Radicals*, ix–x.

97 **"calculated, deliberate, directive, and effective":** Alinsky, *Reveille for Radicals*, x.

99 **"in guiding vote choice":** Barbara Lee Family Foundation and the Center for American Women and Politics, *Finding Gender in Election 2016: Lessons from Presidential Gender Watch* (May 2017), 24.

CHAPTER 13: THERE IS NO WRONG WAY TO BE A WOMAN (*UNITE*)

101 **voted to elect Hillary Clinton:** State Elections Offices, "Official 2016 Presidential General Election Results," January 30, 2017.

101 **in the same age range:** Clare Malone, "Clinton Couldn't Win Over White Women," *FiveThirtyEight*, November 9, 2016.

101 **last four decades holds:** "Gender Differences in Voter Turnout," Center for American Women and Politics.

102 **measuring it fifty years ago:** Danielle Paquette, "The Unexpected Voters Behind the Widest Gender Gap in Recorded Election History," *Washington Post*, November 9, 2016.

102 **"with support for Trump":** Nina Burleigh, "The Presidential Election Was a Referendum on Gender and Women Lost," *Newsweek*, November 14, 2016.

102 **"endemic in our society":** Fareed Zakaria, "Hillary Clinton: Misogyny Is Endemic," *CNN*, October 15, 2017.

102 **"gender and women lost":** Burleigh, "The Presidential Election Was a Referendum."

102 **from voting for him?:** State Elections Offices, "Official 2016 Presidential General Election Results."

102 **"experience didn't matter":** Madigan interview, February 2018.

103 **"both subtle and crystal clear":** Hillary Rodham Clinton, *What Happened* (New York: Simon & Schuster, 2017), 117.

103 **"for the head of state":** Susan Bordo, "Not Until We Can Make Sexism a Public Issue," in "Glass Ceiling: Will America Ever Have a Woman President?" *Politico Magazine*, November/December 2017.

104 **most white men weren't having it:** Matthew Yglesias, "What Really Happened in 2016, in 7 Charts," *Vox*, September 18, 2017.

104 **5.9 million to 9 million people:** German Lopez, "A Year After the First Women's March, Millions Are Still Actively Protesting Trump," *Vox*, January 23, 2018.

104 **Trump-related protests in 2017:** Lopez, "A Year After the First Women's March."

104 **every presidential election since 1964:** "Gender Differences in Voter Turnout," Center for American Women and Politics.

104 **"'Year of the Woman' in American government":** Ariel Scotti, "There Are Over 500 Women Running for Office in 2018," *New York Daily News,* January 29, 2018.

105 **in our nation's history:** Vanessa Williams, "Report: Black Women Underrepresented in Elected Offices, But Could Make Gains and History in 2018," *Washington Post*, March 5, 2018.

105 **to assistant city manager:** "Vi's Experience & Key Accomplishments," Vi Lyles for Mayor website, accessed June 6, 2018.

105 **New Orleans in 2005:** "About LaToya," LaToya Cantrell for Mayor website, accessed June 6, 2018.

105 **out lesbian, Annise Parker:** Krissah Thompson, "Houston's Annise Parker, A Gay Mayor in a Red State, Ponders Political Future," *Washington Post*, March 17, 2015.

105 **elected governor of a formerly Confederate state:** Jonathan Martin and Richard Fausset, "Black, Female and Running for Governor: Can She Win in the South?" *New York Times*, May 19, 2018.

105 **capital of the Confederacy:** Antonio Olivo, "Danica Roem of Virginia to be First Openly Transgender Person Elected, Seated in a U.S. Statehouse," *Washington Post*, November 8, 2017.

105 **Liberian refugee, Wilmot Collins:** Corin Cates-Carney, "How A Liberian Refugee Got To Be A Montana Mayor," NPR, December 25, 2017.

107 **"I don't go to":** Foxx interview, February 2018.

CHAPTER 14: THE FUTURE IS NASTY (*NAME THE ENEMY*)

110 **"legitimate rape":** Lori Moore, "Rep. Todd Akin: The Statement and the Reaction," *New York Times*, August 20, 2012.

110 **"misogynist norms":** Jill Filipovic, "Our President Has Always Degraded Women—And We've Always Let Him," *Time*, December 5, 2017.

110 **"Crooked Hillary":** Ben Geier, "Donald Trump Has a New Nickname for Hillary Clinton," *Fortune*, April 18, 2016.

110 **stiffed his vendors:** Shawn Tully, "Donald Trump Got a Tax Break For Stiffing Contractors," *Fortune*, October 8, 2016.

110 **make those charges go away:** Sudhin Thanawala, "$25M Deal Over Trump University Fraud Lawsuits Moves Forward," Associated Press, February 6, 2018.

112 **through federal funding restrictions:** Ariana Eunjung Cha, "Is it a Gag Rule After All? A Closer Look at Changes to Title X Funding Regarding Abortion," *Washington Post*, May 23, 2018.

112 **"forgiveness is very prominent":** Edward-Isaac Dovere, "Tony Perkins: Trump Gets 'a Mulligan' on Life, Stormy Daniels," *Politico Magazine*, January 23, 2018.

112 **"concern for Christian values":** Dovere, "Tony Perkins: Trump Gets."

112 **"tiptoeing away":** Michael Tackett, "White Evangelical Women, Core Supporters of Trump, Begin Tiptoeing Away," *New York Times*, March 11, 2018.

113 **"not electing a woman president":** Foxx interview, February 2018.

114 **"even to the wages she earns":** "Declaration of Sentiments," National Park Service, accessed January 9, 2018.

114 **"should not be granted to her":** J. B. Sanford, "Argument Against Women's Suffrage," *California State Archives: Secretary of State Elections Papers*, 1922 Special Election.

115 **"to secure her rights":** Sanford, "Argument Against Women's Suffrage."

116 **to reach parity:** Hannah Golden, "Women Are Running Campaigns to Get Women Elected in 2018 & It's Fantastic," *Elite Daily*, February 16, 2018.

CHAPTER 15: IT IS TIME TO USE OUR OUTSIDE VOICES (*SPEAK*)

121 **"our democracy is at stake":** Poo, "A Woman's Work Is Never Done," 70.

121 **"a chance to change the world":** "Dolores Huerta Quotes," AZ Quotes, accessed January 31, 2018.

122 **"we have no voice or representation":** "Abigail Adams Urges Husband to 'Remember the Ladies,'" History.

123 **"that does not serve us well":** Gabriella Paiella, "Janelle Monáe's Powerful Grammys Speech Was All About #TimesUp," *Vulture*, January 28, 2018.

124 **"speak and lead":** Anna Valencia, (Chicago city clerk), interview by the author, February 2018.

124 **"keep your word":** Valencia interview, February 2018.

CHAPTER 16: I AM NOT FREE WHILE ANY WOMAN IS UNFREE (*CONNECT*)

128 **convince New York to ratify:** "Primary Documents in American History: The Federalist Papers," Library of Congress.

128 **which he termed "factions":** *The Federalist Papers:* No. 10, the Avalon Project at Yale Law School.

128 **loose confederation of sovereign states:** "Creating the United States: Road to the Constitution," Library of Congress.

129 **"gender dynamics in the 2016 presidential election":** Barbara Lee Family Foundation and the Center for American Women and Politics, *Finding Gender in Election 2016*, 2.

129 **"whom is deemed presidential":** Barbara Lee Family Foundation and the Center for American Women and Politics, *Finding Gender in Election 2016*, 29.

CHAPTER 17: RESPECT EXISTENCE OR EXPECT RESISTANCE (*RESIST*)

133 **"moving toward justice for all":** "'Resist' Is a Battle Cry, but What Does It Mean?" *New York Times*, February 14, 2017.

134 **advocates children's health:** Katie Rogers, "Melania Trump Rolls Out 'Be Best,' a Children's Agenda With a Focus on Social Media," *New York Times*, May 7, 2018.

134 **Children's Health Insurance Program:** Susannah Luthi, "White House asks Congress to pare back $7 billion from CHIP," *Modern Healthcare*, May 7, 2018.

134 ***The Zookeeper's Wife: A War Story:*** Diane Ackerman, *The Zookeeper's Wife: A War Story* (New York: W. W. Norton & Company, 2007).

134 **Edith Hahn Beer with Susan Dworkin:** Edith Hahn Beer with Susan Dworkin, *The Nazi Officer's Wife: How One Jewish Woman Survived the Holocaust* (New York: William Morrow and Company, 1999).

136 **"based solely on their sex and gender":** Victoria E. Collins, *State Crime, Women and Gender* (New York: Routledge, 2016), 169.

137 **against segregation on interstate buses:** "Freedom Rides," *Encyclopaedia Britannica*.

137 **students to become political activists:** William Sturkey, "The 1964 Mississippi Freedom Schools," *Mississippi History Now*, May 2016.

137 **resistance to racism was on the agenda:** "Mavis Staples Biography," Biography.com, accessed January 16, 2018.

138 **"but he acts like one":** Greg Kot, "Mavis Staples Back on the Freedom Highway: 'It's Like We Have to Start All Over Again,'" *Chicago Tribune*, November 11, 2017.

CHAPTER 18: NOT AFRAID (*FIGHT*)

143 **"police abuse of people of color":** Equal Justice Initiative, *Lynching in America: Confronting the Legacy of Racial Terror,* 2017.

143 **Donald Trump condones:** David Leonhardt and Ian Prasad Philbrick, "Donald Trump's Racism: The Definitive List," *New York Times,* January 15, 2018.

143 **"And then fight like a girl":** Bomshel, "Fight Like a Girl," AZLyrics.com, accessed May 30, 2018.

144 **to both House and Senate seats:** "Smith, Margaret Chase," US House of Representatives History, Art & Archives, accessed February 5, 2018.

144 **won convincingly then and thereafter:** "Smith, Margaret Chase," US House of Representatives History, Art & Archives.

145 **been elected since 1992:** Drew DeSilver, "Women have long history in Congress, but until recently there haven't been many," Pew Research Center, January 14, 2015.

145 **Senate three more times:** "Smith, Margaret Chase," US House of Representatives History, Art & Archives.

146 **"it is not exercised by others":** Margaret Chase Smith, "Declaration of Conscience," US Senate, June 1, 1950.

146 **"fear, bigotry, ignorance and intolerance":** "Smith, Margaret Chase," US House of Representatives History, Art & Archives.

146 **"you kind of like to try":** "Smith, Margaret Chase," US House of Representatives History, Art & Archives.

146 **nomination for the presidency:** "Smith, Margaret Chase," US House of Representatives History, Art & Archives.

147 **"sets the tone and culture":** Foxx interview, February 2018.

CHAPTER 19: I'M WITH HER (*BELIEVE*)

149 **Clinton's 2016 campaign slogan:** Meg Miller, "The Story Behind 'I'm With Her,'" *Co.Design,* April 11, 2017.

149 **symbol of the American Revolution:** Erick Trickey, "The Story Behind a Forgotten Symbol of the American Revolution: The Liberty Tree," Smithsonian. com, May 19, 2016.

149 **raising funds to build a pedestal:** "Statue History: Engineering, Construction, and Crossing the Atlantic," The Statue of Liberty–Ellis Island Foundation.

151 **"They blasted protest speeches":** Vi-An Nguyen, "10 Things You Didn't Know about the Statue of Liberty (She Was Almost Gold!)," *Parade,* July 2, 2014.

151 **through Ellis Island:** Nguyen, "10 Things You Didn't Know."

152 **"part of the great American story":** "Read: Michelle Obama's Speech at 2016 Democratic National Convention," NPR, July 26, 2016.

152 **"yearning to breathe free'":** Emma Lazarus, "The New Colossus," National Park Service, November 2, 1883.

153 **is not really the truth:** Glenn Kessler, Meg Kelly, and Nicole Lewis, "President Trump Has Made 1,628 False or Misleading Claims Over 298 Days," *Washington Post*, November 14, 2017.

CHAPTER 20: MAKE AMERICA THINK AGAIN (*EDUCATE*)

155 **if that partner was a white man:** Lucia Graves, "Why Hillary Clinton Was Right about White Women—and Their Husbands," *Guardian*, September 25, 2017.

156 **(56 percent to 36 percent, respectively):** Julie Kohler, "The Reasons Why White Women Vote Republican—and What to Do about It," *Nation*, February 1, 2018.

156 **"his promises to save American jobs":** Renee Elliott, "Commentary: I Was Betrayed by Donald Trump," *Chicago Tribune*, February 2, 2018.

157 **just 27 percent did so in January 2018:** Eugene Scott, "White Women Helped Elect Trump. Now He's Losing Their Support," *Washington Post*, January 22, 2018.

157 **have continued to deteriorate:** Greg Sargent, "Trump's New Female Accusers May Put Him in Greater Danger," *Washington Post*, March 22, 2018.

157 **89 percent of black voters did:** "2016 Election Exit Polls," *Washington Post*, November 29, 2016.

157 **most invidious of ways:** Clyde Haberman, "George Wallace Tapped into Racial Fear. Decades Later, Its Force Remains Potent," *New York Times*, April 1, 2018.

157 **black women getting the vote:** Sabrina Ford, "How Racism Split the Suffrage Movement," *Bust*, accessed February 5, 2018.

158 **"just as bad as it was before":** Ford, "How Racism Split the Suffrage Movement."

158 **"That's on all of us":** Scott, "White Women Helped Elect Trump."

158 **"recoiled from Republicans":** Alexander Burns and Alan Blinder, "'They Can't Wait to Vote': Energized Democrats Target Dominant GOP in Statehouses," *New York Times*, February 3, 2018.

160 **much of its manufacturing abroad:** "Whirlpool Corporation: Global Locations," Whirlpool Corporation website.

160 **the day before the general election:** Heidi M. Przybyla, "Hillary Clinton Adds Michigan Stop to Campaign Schedule," *USA Today*, November 5, 2016.

CHAPTER 21: WORDS MATTER (*WRITE*)

163 ***Guía para las Mujeres de Chicago:*** Inforwomen, *Chicago Women's Directory*.

164 ***Our Bodies, Ourselves:*** Boston Women's Health Book Collective, *Our Bodies, Ourselves* (Boston, MA: New England Free Press, 1971).

164 ***Women's Yellow Pages:*** Boston Women's Collective, *Women's Yellow Pages: The Original Source Book for Women* (Boston, MA: Boston Women's Collective, Inc., 1973).

164 **"have real substance and meaning":** Inforwomen, *Chicago Women's Directory / Guía para las Mujeres de Chicago:* 59–61.

164 ***What Is to Be Done? Burning Questions of Our Movement:*** Vladimir Ilyich Lenin, *What Is to Be Done? Burning Questions of Our Movement* (1901).

165 **takeover of the Russian government:** Albert Resis, "Vladimir Lenin," *Encyclopaedia Britannica,* last updated April 15, 2018.

165 **"interrelations between *all* classes":** Lenin, *What Is to Be Done?*

166 **"what you can do for your country":** John F. Kennedy, "Inaugural Address," January 20, 1961.

166 **courageous acts stemming from them:** Ted Conover, "The Strike That Brought MLK to Memphis," *Smithsonian,* January 2018.

166 **Yes, we can:** Carolina Moreno, "How Dolores Huerta Inspired Barack Obama's 'Yes We Can' Slogan," *HuffPost,* August 17, 2017.

CHAPTER 22: WE'LL SEE YOU IN COURT (*LITIGATE*)

169 **Supreme Court Justice Ruth Bader Ginsburg:** Dahlia Lithwick, "Justice LOLZ Grumpycat Notorious RBG," *Slate,* March 16, 2015.

169 **Special Committee on Sex and the Law:** The Association of the Bar of the City of New York, *Year Book 1974* (New York, 1974).

169 **(ACLU) Women's Rights Project:** American Civil Liberties Union, "ACLU History: A Driving Force for Change: The ACLU Women's Rights Project," ACLU.org.

170 **"bring me five more":** Sonia Sotomayor, book talk at the Chicago Bar Association, January 30, 2013, as recorded in the author's notes.

170 **Notorious RBG Tumblr:** Lithwick, "Justice LOLZ Grumpycat Notorious RBG."

172 **"Timeline of Major Supreme Court Decisions on Women's Rights":** American Civil Liberties Union, "Timeline of Major Supreme Court Decisions on Women's Rights," last updated 2017.

172 **similarly situated man would be:** *Phillips v. Martin Marietta Corp.,* 400 U.S. 542 (1971).

172 **Abortion is constitutionally protected:** *Roe v. Wade,* 410 U.S. 113 (1973).

172 **Unmarried people can obtain contraception:** *Eisenstadt v. Baird,* 405 U.S. 438 (1972).

173 **must be paid the same wage:** *Corning Glass Works v. Brennan,* 417 U.S. 188 (1974).

173 **jury service on an equal basis:** *Taylor v. Louisiana,* 419 U.S. 522 (1975).

173 **assumptions of dependency:** *Califano v. Goldfarb,* 430 U.S. 199 (1977).

173 **"'dissent' collar":** Lydia Wheeler, "Ginsburg Appears to Wear 'Dissent' Collar on Bench," *Hill,* November 9, 2016.

173 **after Donald Trump's election:** Wheeler, "Ginsburg Appears to Wear 'Dissent' Collar on Bench."

173 **"the ACA would otherwise secure":** *Burwell v. Hobby Lobby Stores, Inc.,* 573 U.S. 2 ___ (2014).

CHAPTER 23: WE ARE IN THIS TOGETHER (*ELECT YOURSELF*)

180 **"own your own destiny":** Valencia interview, February 2018.

180 **"obstructionist to women":** Foxx interview, February 2018.

180 **given birth while in office:** Daniella Diaz and Sunlen Serfaty, "Tammy Duckworth Gives Birth, First US Senator to Do So While in Office," *CNN*, April 9, 2018.

181 **baby in arms:** Saba Hamedy and Daniella Diaz, "Sen. Duckworth Makes History, Casts Vote With Baby on Senate Floor," *CNN*, April 20, 2018.

181 **"why my agenda makes sense":** Valencia interview, February 2018.

182 **have ambitions like yours:** Madigan interview, February 2018.

182 **"I see it, so I can be it":** Foxx interview, February 2018.

182 **continue to meet monthly:** Valencia interview, February 2018.

183 **make such erroneous statements:** Valencia interview, February 2018.

183 **"not about my own ego":** Madigan interview, February 2018.

183 **just as their male counterparts have:** Foxx interview, February 2018.

184 **"through the eyes of being a woman":** Foxx interview, February 2018.

184 **"gotten the positions I wanted":** Valencia interview, February 2018.

184 **emerge as a temporary victor:** Madigan interview, February 2018.

184 **including the presidency:** Madigan interview, February 2018.

185 **expressed interest in running for office:** EMILY's List, "Over 34,000 Women Want to Run for Office."

185 **run for office now or in the future!:** Alicia Menendez, "How & Why Trump's Election Got Women So Psyched about Politics," *Bustle*, April 5, 2018.

CONCLUSION: WOMEN TOGETHER FORWARD

188 **across 106 nations:** World Economic Forum, *The Global Gender Gap Report 2017*, November 2, 2017, viii.

188 **"in Congress and President Trump's cabinet":** Lydia Dishman, "It Will Now Take 100 Years to Reach Gender Equality," *Fast Company*, November 2, 2017.

188 **reach congressional gender equality:** Christianna Silva, "Don't Hold Your Breath for Gender Parity in Congress—It Could Take Another 100 Years," *FiveThirtyEight*, October 3, 2016.

189 **in just three states:** "2018 Summary of Women Candidates," Center for American Women and Politics, last updated May 29, 2018.

189 **none are running for governor:** "2018 Summary of Women Candidates," Center for American Women and Politics.

189 **governors are up for reelection:** "2018 Summary of Women Candidates," Center for American Women and Politics.

189 **ever before in our nation's history:** Tumulty, "'If We Don't Run, Then We Won't Achieve.'"

189 **seventeen of the twenty races:** Steven Shepard, Elena Schneider, and Scott Bland, "Top Takeaways from the First Big Primary of 2018," *Politico*, May 9, 2018.

189 **"a transformation has already begun":** Charlotte Alter, "A Year Ago, They Marched. Now a Record Number of Women Are Running for Office," *Time*, January 18, 2018.

RESOURCES

191 **"I cannot stop fighting":** The Guerrilla Girls, *The Guerrilla Girls' Bedside Companion to the History of Western Art* (New York: Penguin Books, 1998), 70.

BIBLIOGRAPHY

"2016 Election Exit Polls." *Washington Post*, November 29, 2016. https://www
.washingtonpost.com/graphics/politics/2016-election/exit-polls/.

"*2018 Summary of Women Candidates*." Center for American Women and Politics. Last
updated May 29, 2018. http://cawp.rutgers.edu/potential-candidate-summary-2018.

"Abigail Adams Urges Husband to 'Remember the Ladies.'" History. http://www.history
.com/this-day-in-history/abigail-adams-urges-husband-to-remember-the-ladies.

"About LaToya." LaToya Cantrell for Mayor website. Accessed June 6, 2018.
https://latoyacantrell.com/biography/.

Ackerman, Diane. *The Zookeeper's Wife: A War Story*. New York: W. W. Norton &
Company, 2007.

Addams, Jane. *Twenty Years at Hull-House With Autobiographical Notes*. New York:
New American Library, Third Printing, 1961.

"Addie Wyatt: UFCW Lighthouse." United Food and Commercial Workers Union Local
324, April 9, 1952. https://ufcw324.org/addie-wyatt-ufcw-lighthouse/.

"African American Reformers: The Club Movement." National Women's History
Museum. https://www.nwhm.org/resources/general/african-american-reformers.

Alinsky, Saul. *Reveille for Radicals*. New York: Vintage Books, 1969.

Alter, Charlotte. "A Year Ago, They Marched. Now a Record Number of Women Are
Running for Office." *Time*, January 18, 2018. http://time.com/5107499/record
-number-of-women-are-running-for-office/.

American Civil Liberties Union. "ACLU History: A Driving Force for Change: The ACLU
Women's Rights Project." ACLU.org. https://www.aclu.org/other/aclu-history
-driving-force-change-aclu-womens-rights-project.

American Civil Liberties Union. "Timeline of Major Supreme Court Decisions on
Women's Rights." Last updated 2017. https://www.aclu.org/other/timeline-major
-supreme-court-decisions-womens-rights.

Andersen, David J., and John Weingart. "Governors Who Became President." Rutgers University Eagleton Institute of Politics Center on the American Governor, 2014. http://governors.rutgers.edu/on-governors/us-governors/governors-and-the-white -house/governors-who-became-president/.

Andrews, Inez, vocalist. "Lord Don't Move the Mountain" by Doris Akers, *Lord Don't Move the Mountain*. Jewel Records, 1995. Compact disc. https://www.allmusic.com /album/lord-don%E2%80%99t-move-that-mountain-mw0000181331.

Barbara Lee Family Foundation and the Center for American Women and Politics. *Finding Gender in Election 2016: Lessons from Presidential Gender Watch*, May 2017. http://presidentialgenderwatch.org/wp-content/uploads/2017/05/Finding-Gender -in-Election-2016.pdf.

Barron, James. "Shirley Chisholm, 'Unbossed' Pioneer in Congress, Is Dead at 80." *New York Times*, January 3, 2005. http://www.nytimes.com/2005/01/03/obituaries /shirley-chisholm-unbossedpioneer-in-congress-is-dead-at-80.html.

Beard, Mary. *Women & Power: A Manifesto*. New York: Liveright Publishing Corporation, 2017.

Beer, Edith Hahn, with Susan Dworkin. *The Nazi Officer's Wife: How One Jewish Woman Survived the Holocaust*. New York: William Morrow and Company, 1999.

Bennett, Jessica. "Girls Can Be Anything, Just Not President." *New York Times*, November 10, 2016. https://www.nytimes.com/2016/11/10/opinion/girls-can-be -anything-just-not-president.html.

Beyoncé. "Formation." *Lemonade*. Columbia Records, 2016. Compact disc.

Beyoncé. "Run the World (Girls)." *4*. Columbia Records, 2011. Compact disc.

Bialik, Kristen. "Americans Deepest in Poverty Lost More Ground in 2016." Pew Research Center, October 6, 2017. http://www.pewresearch.org/fact-tank/2017 /10/06/americans-deepest-in-poverty-lost-more-ground-in-2016/.

"Black History Month: Addie Wyatt." United Food and Commercial Workers Union Local 324, February 15, 2018. http://www.ufcw.org/2018/02/15/black-history-month -addie-wyatt/.

Bomshel. "Fight Like a Girl." AZLyrics.com. Accessed May 30, 2018. https://www.azlyrics .com/lyrics/bomshel/fightlikeagirl.html.

Bordo, Susan. "Not Until We Can Make Sexism a Public Issue." In "Glass Ceiling: Will America Ever Have a Woman President?" *Politico Magazine*, November/December 2017. https://www.politico.com/magazine/story/2017/11/03/will-america-have -woman-president-politics-2017-215769.

Boston Women's Collective, *Women's Yellow Pages: The Original Source Book for Women*. Boston, MA: Boston Women's Collective, Inc., 1973.

Boston Women's Health Book Collective, *Our Bodies, Ourselves*. Boston, MA: New England Free Press, 1971.

Brechenmacher, Saskia. "Tackling Women's Underrepresentation in US Politics: Comparative Perspectives from Europe." Carnegie Endowment for International Peace, February 20, 2018. https://carnegieendowment.org/2018/02/20/tackling -women-s-underrepresentation-in-u.s.-politics-comparative-perspectives-from -europe-pub-75315.

Brownstein, Ronald. "White Women in the Rustbelt Are Turning on Trump." *Atlantic*, February 8, 2018. https://www.theatlantic.com/politics/archive/2018/02/trump -approval-rating-2018-midterms/552701/.

Burleigh, Nina. "The Presidential Election Was a Referendum on Gender and Women Lost." *Newsweek*, November 14, 2016. http://www.newsweek.com/2016/11/18 /hillary-clinton-presidential-election-voter-gender-gap-520579.html.

Burns, Alexander, and Alan Blinder. "'They Can't Wait to Vote': Energized Democrats Target Dominant GOP in Statehouses." *New York Times*, February 3, 2018. https://www.nytimes.com/2018/02/03/us/politics/state-elections-midterms.html.

Burwell v. Hobby Lobby Stores, Inc., 573 U.S. 2 ___ (2014).

Bush v. Gore, 531 U.S. 98 (2000).

"But Can She Type? [Golda Meir]." Library of Congress, ca. 1970. http://www.loc.gov /pictures/item/99471825/.

Calamur, Krishnadev. "A Short History of 'America First.'" *Atlantic*, January 21, 2017. https://www.theatlantic.com/politics/archive/2017/01/trump-america-first/514037.

Califano v. Goldfarb, 430 U.S. 199 (1977).

Cates-Carney, Corin. "How A Liberian Refugee Got To Be A Montana Mayor." NPR, December 25, 2017. https://www.npr.org/sections/goatsandsoda/2017/12/25 /572835450/how-a-liberian-refugee-got-to-be-a-montana-mayor.

Caygle, Heather. "Record-Breaking Number of Women Run for Office." *Politico*, March 8, 2018. https://www.politico.com/story/2018/03/08/women-rule-midterms-443267.

Cha, Ariana Eunjung. "Is it a Gag Rule After All? A Closer Look at Changes to Title X Funding Regarding Abortion." *Washington Post*, May 23, 2018. https://www .washingtonpost.com/news/to-your-health/wp/2018/05/23/is-it-a-gag-rule-what -changes-to-family-planning-funds-and-abortion-referrals-might-mean.

"Chisholm, Shirley Anita." US House of Representatives History, Art & Archives. Accessed April 1, 2018. http://history.house.gov/People/Detail/10918.

Clines, Francis X. "Trump Quits Grand Old Party for New." *New York Times*, October 25, 1999. http://articles.orlandosentinel.com/1999-10-25/news/9910250078_1_reform -party-trump-buchanan.

Clinton, Chelsea. *She Persisted: 13 American Women Who Changed the World*. New York: Philomel Books, 2017.

Clinton, Hillary Rodham. *What Happened*. New York: Simon & Schuster, 2017.

Cohen, Nancy L. *Breakthrough: The Making of America's First Woman President*. Berkeley, CA: Counterpoint, 2016.

Collins, Victoria E. *State Crime, Women and Gender*. New York: Routledge, 2016.

Conover, Ted. "The Strike That Brought MLK to Memphis." *Smithsonian*, January 2018. https://www.smithsonianmag.com/history/revisiting-sanitation-workers-strike -180967512/.

Cormack, Lindsey. "Gender and Vote Revelation Strategy in the United States Congress." *Journal of Gender Studies* 25, no. 6 (Summer 2015): 626–640. https://doi.org/10.1080 /09589236.2015.1078228.

Corning Glass Works v. Brennan, 417 U.S. 188 (1974).

"Creating the United States: Road to the Constitution." Library of Congress. https://www
.loc.gov/exhibits/creating-the-united-states/road-to-the-constitution.html.

"Declaration of Sentiments." National Park Service. Accessed January 9, 2018.
https://www.nps.gov/wori/learn/historyculture/declaration-of-sentiments.htm.

DeSilver, Drew. "Women have long history in Congress, but until recently there haven't
been many." Pew Research Center, January 14, 2015. http://www.pewresearch.org
/fact-tank/2015/01/14/women-have-long-history-in-congress-but-until-recently
-there-havent-been-many/.

DeWolf, Mark. "12 Stats about Working Women." US Department of Labor blog,
March 1, 2017. https://blog.dol.gov/2017/03/01/12-stats-about-working-women.

Diaz, Daniella, and Sunlen Serfaty. "Tammy Duckworth Gives Birth, First US Senator to
Do So While in Office." *CNN*, April 9, 2018. https://www.cnn.com/2018/04/09
/politics/tammy-duckworth-gives-birth-baby-girl/index.html.

Dishman, Lydia. "It Will Now Take 100 Years to Reach Gender Equality." *Fast Company*,
November 2, 2017. https://www.fastcompany.com/40490716/it-will-now-take-100
-years-to-reach-gender-equality.

Dittmar, Kelly. "A Different Measure of Success for Women Running in 2018." Gender
Watch 2018, March 28, 2018. https://www.genderwatch2018.org/success/.

Dittmar, Kelly. "After #SuperTuesday Primaries, Women Candidates on Path to
Make History in Multiple States." Gender Watch 2018, June 6, 2018. https://
www.genderwatch2018.org/primary-results-june-5/.

"Dolores Huerta Quotes." AZ Quotes. Accessed January 31, 2018. http://www.azquotes
.com/author/22152-Dolores_Huerta.

Dovere, Edward-Isaac. "Tony Perkins: Trump Gets 'a Mulligan' on Life, Stormy Daniels."
Politico Magazine, January 23, 2018. https://www.politico.com/magazine/story
/2018/01/23/tony-perkins-evangelicals-donald-trump-stormy-daniels-216498.

Doyle, Kevin. "Hillary Clinton Rarely Listens to Her iPod, Always Packs Tabasco Sauce."
Condé Nast Traveler, August 30, 2012. https://www.cntraveler.com/stories/2012-08
-30/hillary-clinton-interview-visionaries.

Dunham, Richard. "What Went Wrong for Hillary Clinton." *Houston Chronicle*, June 3,
2008. https://www.chron.com/news/nation-world/article/What-went-wrong-for
-Hillary-Clinton-1670043.php.

Eisenstadt v. Baird, 405 U.S. 438 (1972).

Elliott, Renee. "Commentary: I Was Betrayed by Donald Trump." *Chicago Tribune*,
February 2, 2018. http://www.chicagotribune.com/news/opinion/commentary
/ct-perspec-carrier-jobs-trump-0205-story.html.

EMILY's List. "Over 34,000 Women Want to Run for Office." Press release, February 27,
2018. https://www.emilyslist.org/news/entry/over-34000-women-want-to-run
-for-office.

Equal Justice Initiative. *Lynching in America: Confronting the Legacy of Racial Terror*,
2017. https://eji.org/reports/lynching-in-america.

Faludi, Susan. "The Patriarchs Are Falling. The Patriarchy Is Stronger Than Ever."
New York Times, December 28, 2017. https://www.nytimes.com/2017/12/28/opinion
/sunday/patriarchy-feminism-metoo.html.

Fausset, Richard, and Mitch Smith. "Megan Barry, Nashville Mayor, Pleads Guilty to Theft and Agrees to Resign." *New York Times*, March 6, 2018. https://www.nytimes .com/2018/03/06/us/megan-barry-nashville.html.

The Federalist Papers: No. 10. The Avalon Project at Yale Law School. http://avalon.law .yale.edu/18th_century/fed10.asp.

Filipovic, Jill. "Our President Has Always Degraded Women—And We've Always Let Him." *Time*, December 5, 2017. http://time.com/5047771/donald-trump-comments -billy-bush/.

Fitzsimmons, Emma Graves. "Florence Scala: 1918–2007." *Chicago Tribune*, August 29, 2007. http://articles.chicagotribune.com/2007-08-29/news/0708281426_1_hull -house-city-hall-studs-terkel.

Foerstel, Karen, and Herbert N. Foerstel. *Climbing the Hill: Gender Conflict in Congress*. Westport, CT: Praeger, 1996.

Foran, Clare. "Women Aren't Responsible for Hillary Clinton's Defeat." *Atlantic*, November 13, 2016. https://www.theatlantic.com/politics/archive/2016/11 /hillary-clinton-white-women-vote/507422/.

Ford, Sabrina. "How Racism Split the Suffrage Movement." *Bust*. Accessed February 5, 2018. http://bust.com/feminism/19147-equal-means-equal.html.

Foxx, Kimberly M. (Cook County, Illinois, state's attorney). Interview by the author, February 2018.

"Freedom Rides." *Encyclopaedia Britannica*. https://www.britannica.com/event /Freedom-Rides.

Freeman, Jo. "Shirley Chisholm's 1972 Presidential Campaign." University of Illinois at Chicago Women's Political History Project, February 2005, archived from the original on November 11, 2014. https://web.archive.org/web/20141111182057 /http:/www.uic.edu/orgs/cwluherstory/jofreeman/polhistory/chisholm.htm.

Fritze, John, and Alison Knezevich. "President Trump: 'From This Day Forward It's Only Going to Be America First.'" *Baltimore Sun*, January 20, 2017. http://www .baltimoresun.com/news/nation-world/politics/bs-md-trump-inauguration -20170120-story.html.

Frost, Amber. "Bring Back the Feminists of WITCH (Women's International Terrorist Conspiracy from Hell)!" *Dangerous Minds*, February 6, 2015. https://dangerousminds .net/comments/bring_back_the_feminists_of_witch.

Fry, Richard. "Millennials Projected to Overtake Baby Boomers as America's Largest Generation." Pew Research Center, March 1, 2018. http://www.pewresearch.org /fact-tank/2018/03/01/millennials-overtake-baby-boomers/.

Geier, Ben. "Donald Trump Has a New Nickname for Hillary Clinton." *Fortune*, April 18, 2016. http://fortune.com/2016/04/18/trump-clinton-nickname/.

"Gender Differences in Voter Turnout." Center for American Women and Politics, July 20, 2017. http://www.cawp.rutgers.edu/sites/default/files/resources/genderdiff.pdf.

Goings, Kenneth W. "Memphis Free Speech." *Tennessee Encyclopedia of History and Culture*, October 8, 2017. http://tennesseeencyclopedia.net/entry.php?rec=894.

Gold, Bertram H. "Who Speaks for the Jews." Text of address by Gold, executive vice president of the American Jewish Committee, at the committee's annual meeting, New York City, May 4, 1972. Cited in Arthur A. Goren. *The Politics and Public Culture of American Jews: The Modern Jewish Experience.* Bloomington: Indiana University Press, 1999.

Goldberg, Michelle. "Season of the Witch." *New York Times*, November 3, 2017. https://www.nytimes.com/2017/11/03/opinion/witches-occult-comeback.html.

Golden, Hannah. "Women Are Running Campaigns to Get Women Elected in 2018 & It's Fantastic." *Elite Daily*, February 16, 2018. https://www.elitedaily.com/p/women-are-running-campaigns-to-get-women-elected-in-2018-its-fantastic-exclusive-8181712.

Gordon-Reed, Annette. "Female Trouble." *New York Review of Books*, February 8, 2018. http://www.nybooks.com/articles/2018/02/08/hillary-clinton-female-trouble.

Gore, Lesley. "You Don't Own Me." Mercury Records, 1963. Seven-inch single.

Graves, Lucia. "Why Hillary Clinton Was Right about White Women—and Their Husbands." *Guardian*, September 25, 2017. https://www.theguardian.com/us-news/2017/sep/25/white-women-husbands-voting.

Greenstone, Michael, and Adam Looney. "The Marriage Gap: The Impact of Economic and Technological Change on Marriage Rates." The Hamilton Project at the Brookings Institution, February 3, 2012. https://www.brookings.edu/blog/jobs/2012/02/03/the-marriage-gap-the-impact-of-economic-and-technological-change-on-marriage-rates/.

The Guerilla Girls. *The Guerilla Girls' Bedside Companion to the History of Western Art.* New York: Penguin Books, 1998.

H., Jessica. "They Tried to Bury Us. They Didn't Know We Were Seeds." *J.H. Fearless* (blog), November 24, 2014. http://jhfearless.com/2014/11/they-tried-to-bury-us-they-didnt-know-we-were-seeds/.

Haberman, Clyde. "George Wallace Tapped into Racial Fear. Decades Later, Its Force Remains Potent." *New York Times*, April 1, 2018. https://www.nytimes.com/2018/04/01/us/george-wallace-tapped-into-racial-fear-decades-later-its-force-remains-potent.html.

Hamedy, Saba, and Daniella Diaz. "Sen. Duckworth Makes History, Casts Vote With Baby on Senate Floor." *CNN*, April 20, 2018. https://www.cnn.com/2018/04/19/politics/tammy-duckworth-baby-senate-floor/index.html.

Hill, James. "West Side Inspiration Nancy Jefferson, 69." *Chicago Tribune*, October 19, 1992. http://articles.chicagotribune.com/1992-10-19/news/9204040604_1_mrs-jefferson-west-siders-chicago-alderman.

"Historical Summary of Women in Statewide Elective Executive Office: 1969–Current." Center for American Women and Politics. http://www.cawp.rutgers.edu/historical-summary-women-statewide-elective-executive-office-1969-current.

"Historic Gender Gap Isn't Enough to Propel Clinton to Victory in 2016 Presidential Race." Center for American Women and Politics, November 9, 2016. http://cawp.rutgers.edu/sites/default/files/resources/post-election-gg-release-2016-presidential.pdf.

"History of Women in the US Congress." Center for American Women and Politics. Last updated 2018. http://www.cawp.rutgers.edu/history-women-us-congress.

Holter, Lauren. "Governor Races in 2018 Could See More Women Running Than Ever Before." *Bustle*, January 2, 2018. https://www.bustle.com/p/governor-races-in-2018 -could-see-more-women-running-than-ever-before-7745667.

Hunt, Swanee, and Andrea Dew Steele. "A Seismic Shift in Government Is Coming, and Here's Who Will Drive It." *CNN*, April 21, 2018. https://www.cnn.com/2018/01/02 /opinions/women-representation-opinion-hunt-steele/index.html.

"Ida B. Wells Biography." Biography.com. Accessed January 16, 2018. https://www .biography.com/people/ida-b-wells-9527635.

Inforwomen. *Chicago Women's Directory / Guía para las Mujeres de Chicago*. Chicago, 1974.

"International Civil Rights Walk of Fame: Addie L. Wyatt." National Park Service. Accessed January 9, 2018. https://www.nps.gov/features/malu/feat0002/wof /Addie_Wyatt.htm.

"Jane Addams – Biographical." Nobelprize.org. From *Nobel Lectures, Peace 1926–1950*. Editor Frederick W. Haberman. Amsterdam: Elsevier Publishing Company, 1972. https://www.nobelprize.org/nobel_prizes/peace/laureates/1931/addams-bio.html.

Jane Addams Hull-House Museum website. Accessed April 1, 2018. https://www .hullhousemuseum.org/.

Janu, Bruce D., and Wendy Hamand Venet. "Mary Livermore and the Illinois Women's Suffrage Movement." Illinois Periodicals Online. Accessed January 16, 2018. http://www.lib.niu.edu/1996/iht319602.html.

Kennedy, John F. "Inaugural Address." January 20, 1961. https://millercenter.org /the-presidency/presidential-speeches/january-20-1961-inaugural-address.

Kessler, Glenn, Meg Kelly, and Nicole Lewis. "President Trump Has Made 1,628 False or Misleading Claims Over 298 Days." *Washington Post*, November 14, 2017. https://www .washingtonpost.com/news/fact-checker/wp/2017/11/14/president-trump-has-made -1628-false-or-misleading-claims-over-298-days/.

Kohler, Julie. "The Reasons Why White Women Vote Republican—and What to Do about It." *Nation*, February 1, 2018. https://www.thenation.com/article/the-reasons-why -white-women-vote-republican-and-what-to-do-about-it/.

Kosoff, Maya. "Can Millennial Women Decide the Next Election?" *Vanity Fair*, February 27, 2018. https://www.vanityfair.com/news/2018/02/can-millennial-women -decide-the-next-election.

Kot, Greg. "Mavis Staples Back on the Freedom Highway: 'It's Like We Have to Start All Over Again.'" *Chicago Tribune*, November 11, 2017. http://www.chicagotribune.com /entertainment/music/ct-ae-mavis-staples-tweedy-1112-story.html.

Krieg, Gregory. "It's Official: Clinton Swamps Trump in Popular Vote." *CNN*, December 22, 2016. https://www.cnn.com/2016/12/21/politics/donald-trump-hillary-clinton -popular-vote-final-count/index.html.

Kuttner, Robert. "Hidden Injuries of Class, Race, and Culture." *American Prospect*, October 3, 2016. http://prospect.org/article/hidden-injuries-0.

Landsbaum, Claire. "Most Low-Wage Workers in the United States Are Women, Study Finds." *The Cut*, December 28, 2016. https://www.thecut.com/2016/12/most-low-wage-workers-are-women-study-finds.html.

Lazarus, Emma. "The New Colossus." National Park Service. November 2, 1883. https://www.nps.gov/stli/learn/historyculture/colossus.htm.

Lenin, Vladimir Ilyich. *What Is to Be Done? Burning Questions of Our Movement.* 1901. https://www.marxists.org/archive/lenin/works/1901/witbd/iii.htm.

Leonhardt, David, and Ian Prasad Philbrick. "Donald Trump's Racism: The Definitive List." *New York Times*, January 15, 2018. https://www.nytimes.com/interactive/2018/01/15/opinion/leonhardt-trump-racist.html.

Levine, Irving M. *The New Pluralism.* National Project on Ethnic America.

Lipman, Joanne. "How Diversity Training Infuriates Men and Fails Women." *Time*, January 25, 2018. http://time.com/5118035/diversity-training-infuriates-men-fails-women/.

Liptak, Adam. "On Tour With Notorious RBG, Judicial Rock Star." *New York Times*, February 8, 2018. https://www.nytimes.com/2018/02/08/us/politics/ruth-bader-ginsburg.html.

Lithwick, Dahlia. "Justice LOLZ Grumpycat Notorious RBG." *Slate*, March 16, 2015. http://www.slate.com/articles/double_x/doublex/2015/03/notorious_r_b_g_history_the_origins_and_meaning_of_ruth_bader_ginsburg_s.html.

Lopez, German. "A Year After the First Women's March, Millions Are Still Actively Protesting Trump." *Vox*, January 23, 2018. https://www.vox.com/policy-and-politics/2018/1/23/16922884/womens-march-attendance.

Luthi, Susannah. "White House Asks Congress to Pare Back $7 Billion from CHIP." *Modern Healthcare*, May 7, 2018. http://www.modernhealthcare.com/article/20180507/NEWS/180509930.

Madigan, Lisa (Illinois attorney general). Interview by the author, February 2018.

"Madonna." *People* archive, July 27, 1992. https://people.com/archive/madonna-vol-38-no-4/.

Malone, Clare. "Clinton Couldn't Win Over White Women." *FiveThirtyEight*, November 9, 2016. https://fivethirtyeight.com/features/clinton-couldn't-win-over-white-women/.

Martin, Jonathan. "Democrats Mount Effort to Recruit Women as State Attorneys General." *New York Times*, September 19, 2017. https://www.nytimes.com/2017/09/19/us/politics/democratic-women-state-attorneys-general.html.

Martin, Jonathan, and Richard Fausset. "Black, Female and Running for Governor: Can She Win in the South?" *New York Times*, May 19, 2018. https://www.nytimes.com/2018/05/19/us/politics/governor-georgia-primary-democrat-stacey-abrams.html.

Martin, Jonathan, and Alexander Burns. "Democratic Women Are Running for Governor. Men and Money Stand in Their Way." *New York Times*, June 11, 2018. https://www.nytimes.com/2018/06/11/us/politics/governor-primary-women-nevada.html.

Martin, Jonathan, and Alexander Burns. "Stacey Abrams Wins Georgia Democratic Primary for Governor, Making History." *New York Times*, May 22, 2018. https://www.nytimes.com/2018/05/22/us/politics/georgia-primary-abrams-results.html.

"Mavis Staples Biography." Biography.com. Accessed January 16, 2018. https://www
    .biography.com/people/mavis-staples-17178794.

Menand, Louis. *The Metaphysical Club: A Story of Ideas in America*. New York: Farrar,
    Straus and Giroux, 2001.

Menendez, Alicia. "How & Why Trump's Election Got Women So Psyched about
    Politics." *Bustle*, April 5, 2018. https://www.bustle.com/p/how-why-trumps-election
    -got-women-so-psyched-about-politics-8702706.

"Milestones for Women in American Politics." Center for American Women and Politics.
    http://www.cawp.rutgers.edu/facts/milestones-for-women.

Miller, Claire Cain. "The Number of Female Chief Executives Is Falling." *New York Times*,
    May 23, 2018. https://www.nytimes.com/2018/05/23/upshot/why-the-number-of
    -female-chief-executives-is-falling.html.

Miller, Claire Cain. "Women Actually Do Govern Differently." *New York Times*,
    November 10, 2016. https://www.nytimes.com/2016/11/10/upshot/women
    -actually-do-govern-differently.html.

Miller, Meg. "The Story Behind 'I'm With Her.'" *Co.Design*, April 11, 2017. https://www
    .fastcodesign.com/90109190/the-story-behind-im-with-her.

Miller, Rich. "Leader Currie to Retire at End of Term." *Capitol Fax*, September 15, 2017.
    https://capitolfax.com/2017/09/15/leader-currie-to-retire-at-end-of-term/.

Mohdin, Aamna. "American Women Voted Overwhelmingly for Clinton, Except the
    White Ones." *Quartz*, November 9, 2016. https://qz.com/833003/election-2016
    -all-women-voted-overwhelmingly-for-clinton-except-the-white-ones/.

Moore, Lori. "Rep. Todd Akin: The Statement and the Reaction." *New York Times*,
    August 20, 2012. https://www.nytimes.com/2012/08/21/us/politics/rep-todd-akin
    -legitimate-rape-statement-and-reaction.html.

Moreno, Carolina. "How Dolores Huerta Inspired Barack Obama's 'Yes We Can' Slogan."
    HuffPost, August 17, 2017. https://www.huffingtonpost.com/entry/how-dolores
    -huerta-inspired-barack-obamas-yes-we-can-slogan_us_5994a999e4b06ef724d60506.

Morgan, Robin, ed. *Sisterhood Is Powerful: An Anthology of Writings from the Women's
    Liberation Movement*. New York: Random House, 1970.

MTV. "Nicki Minaj: 'My Time Now.'" MTV Music Specials, 2010. http://www.mtv.com.au
    /mtv-music-specials/videos/mtv-music-special-nicki-minaj-my-time-now.

National Committee to Draft Oprah Winfrey for President of the United States 2020.
    "Press Release." January 15, 2018. https://yesshecan.democrat/press-release/.

Nguyen, Vi-An. "10 Things You Didn't Know about the Statue of Liberty (She Was Almost
    Gold!)." *Parade*, July 2, 2014. https://parade.com/311395/vianguyen/10-things
    -you-didnt-know-about-the-statue-of-liberty-she-was-almost-gold/.

North, Anna. "Hillary Clinton Has a Theory about Why She Lost With White Women." *Vox*,
    September 12, 2017. https://www.vox.com/policy-and-politics/2017/9/12/16295260
    /hillary-clinton-white-women-sexism-what-happened.

Nsehe, Mfonobong. "The Black Billionaires 2018." *Forbes*, March 7, 2018. https://www
    .forbes.com/sites/mfonobongnsehe/2018/03/07/the-black-billionaires-2018/.

Odlum, Lakisha. "The Black Power Movement." Digital Public Library of America, 2015. https://dp.la/primary-source-sets/the-black-power-movement.

O'Grady, Megan. "*Vogue*'s Fall Books Guide: The Best Books of the Season." *Vogue*, September 9, 2015. https://www.vogue.com/article/fall-2015-books-guide.

"Oldest and Boldest." National Association for the Advancement of Colored People. http://www.naacp.org/oldest-and-boldest/.

Olivo, Antonio. "Danica Roem of Virginia to be First Openly Transgender Person Elected, Seated in a U.S. Statehouse." *Washington Post*, November 8, 2017. https://www.washingtonpost.com/local/virginia-politics/danica-roem-will-be-vas-first-openly-transgender-elected-official-after-unseating-conservative-robert-g-marshall-in-house-race/2017/11/07/d534bdde-c0af-11e7-959c-fe2b598d8c00_story.html?utm_term=.0b9bb8d12c38.

Paiella, Gabriella. "Janelle Monáe's Powerful Grammys Speech Was All About #TimesUp." *Vulture*, January 28, 2018. http://www.vulture.com/2018/01/janelle-mones-powerful-grammys-speech-was-about-timesup.html.

Paquette, Danielle. "The Unexpected Voters Behind the Widest Gender Gap in Recorded Election History." *Washington Post*, November 9, 2016. https://www.washingtonpost.com/news/wonk/wp/2016/11/09/men-handed-trump-the-election.

Parker, Kim, Juliana Menasce Horowitz, Wendy Wang, Anna Brown, and Eileen Patten. "Chapter 3: Obstacles to Female Leadership." *Women and Leadership: Public Says Women Are Equally Qualified, but Barriers Persist*. Pew Research Center, January 14, 2015. http://www.pewsocialtrends.org/2015/01/14/chapter-3-obstacles-to-female-leadership/.

Patten, Eileen. "Racial, Gender Wage Gaps Persist in US Despite Some Progress." Pew Research Center, July 1, 2016. http://www.pewresearch.org/fact-tank/2016/07/01/racial-gender-wage-gaps-persist-in-u-s-despite-some-progress/.

"People Search: Women in Congress, 91st (1969–1971)." US House of Representatives History, Art & Archives. Accessed April 1, 2018. http://history.house.gov/People/Search.

Phillips v. Martin Marietta Corp., 400 U.S. 542 (1971).

Pogrebin, Letty Cottin. "Golda Meir." *Jewish Women: A Comprehensive Historical Encyclopedia*, March 20, 2009. Jewish Women's Archive. https://jwa.org/encyclopedia/article/meir-golda.

Poo, Ai-jen. "A Woman's Work Is Never Done (in a Democracy)." In *Together We Rise: Behind the Scenes at the Protest Heard Around the World*. New York: Dey Street Books, 2018.

"Primary Documents in American History: The Federalist Papers." Library of Congress. http://www.loc.gov/rr/program/bib/ourdocs/federalist.html.

Przybyla, Heidi M. "Hillary Clinton Adds Michigan Stop to Campaign Schedule." *USA Today*, November 5, 2016. https://www.usatoday.com/story/news/politics/onpolitics/2016/11/05/hillary-clinton-michigan/93356788/.

"Read: Michelle Obama's Speech at 2016 Democratic National Convention." NPR, July 26, 2016. https://www.npr.org/2016/07/26/487431756/michelle-obamas-prepared -remarks-for-democratic-national-convention.

"Read Oprah Winfrey's Rousing Golden Globes Speech." *CNN*, January 10, 2018. https://www.cnn.com/2018/01/08/entertainment/oprah-globes-speech-transcript /index.html.

Resis, Albert. "Vladimir Lenin." *Encyclopaedia Britannica*. Last updated April 15, 2018. https://www.britannica.com/biography/Vladimir-Lenin.

"'Resist' Is a Battle Cry, but What Does It Mean?" *New York Times*. February 14, 2017. https://www.nytimes.com/2017/02/14/us/politics/resist-anti-trump-protest.html.

Reynolds, Toby, and Paul Calver. *Fearless Women: Courageous Females Who Refused to Be Denied*. Real Lives series. Hauppauge, NY: Barron's Educational Series, 2017.

Roach, Marilynne K. "9 Reasons You Might Have Been Suspected of Witchcraft in 1692." *HuffPost*, October 2, 2013. https://www.huffingtonpost.com/marilynne-k-roach /9-reasons-you-might-have-_b_4029745.html.

Roe v. Wade, 410 U.S. 113 (1973).

Roemer, Tim. "Why Do Congressmen Spend Only Half Their Time Serving Us?" *Newsweek*, July 29, 2015. http://www.newsweek.com/why-do-congressmen-spend -only-half-their-time-serving-us-357995.

Rogers, Katie. "Melania Trump Rolls Out 'Be Best,' a Children's Agenda With a Focus on Social Media." *New York Times*, May 7, 2018. https://www.nytimes.com/2018/05/07 /us/politics/melania-trump-children.html.

Rothkopf, Joanna. "An Investigation: Which Presidential Campaigns Have the Largest Gender Wage Disparities?" *Jezebel*, March 15, 2016. https://theslot.jezebel.com /an-investigation-which-presidential-campaigns-have-the-1762895557.

Rustin, Susanna. "Can Cities Be Feminist? Inside the Global Rise of Female Mayors." *Guardian*, October 12, 2016. https://www.theguardian.com/cities/2016/oct/12 /global-rise-female-mayors.

Sandberg, Sheryl. *Lean In: Women, Work, and the Will to Lead*. New York: Alfred A. Knopf, 2013.

Sanford, J. B. "Argument Against Women's Suffrage." California State Archives: Secretary of State Elections Papers, 1911 Special Election.

Sargent, Greg. "Trump's New Female Accusers May Put Him in Greater Danger." *Washington Post*, March 22, 2018. https://www.washingtonpost.com/blogs/plum-line /wp/2018/03/22/trumps-new-female-accusers-may-put-him-in-greater-danger/.

Scher, Bill. "Why 2020 Will Be the Year of the Woman." *Politico Magazine*, November 24, 2017. https://www.politico.com/magazine/story/2017/11/24/2020-year-of-woman -democrats-post-weinstein-kamala-harris-klobuchar-gillibrand-warren-215860.

Schiff, Stacy. *The Witches: Suspicion, Betrayal, and Hysteria in 1692 Salem*. New York: Back Bay Books, 2015.

Scott, Anne Firor. "Saint Jane and the Ward Boss." *American Heritage* 12, no. 1, December 1960. https://www.americanheritage.com/content/saint-jane-and-ward-boss.

Scott, Eugene. "White Women Helped Elect Trump. Now He's Losing Their Support." *Washington Post*, January 22, 2018. https://www.washingtonpost.com/news/the-fix /wp/2018/01/22/white-women-helped-elect-trump-now-hes-losing-their-support/.

Scotti, Ariel. "There Are Over 500 Women Running for Office in 2018." *New York Daily News*, January 29, 2018. http://www.nydailynews.com/news/national/500-women -running-office-2018-article-1.3785976.

Seifer, Nancy. *Absent from the Majority: Working Class Women in America*. Middle America pamphlet series. National Project on Ethnic America, 1973.

Seltzer, Rick. "The Slowly Diversifying Presidency." *Inside Higher Ed*, June 20, 2017. https://www.insidehighered.com/news/2017/06/20/college-presidents-diversifying -slowly-and-growing-older-study-finds.

Sennett, Richard, and Jonathan Cobb. *The Hidden Injuries of Class*. New York: Alfred A. Knopf, 1972.

Shaw, Elyse, Ariane Hegewisch, Emma Williams-Baron, and Barbara Gault. *Undervalued and Underpaid in America: Women in Low-Wage, Female-Dominated Jobs*. Institute for Women's Policy Research, November 17, 2016.

Shepard, Steven, Elena Schneider, and Scott Bland. "Top Takeaways from the First Big Primary of 2018." *Politico*, May 9, 2018. https://www.politico.com/story/2018/05/09 /west-virginia-primary-election-results-2018-analysis-576783.

Silva, Christianna. "Don't Hold Your Breath for Gender Parity in Congress – It Could Take Another 100 Years." *FiveThirtyEight*, October 3, 2016. http://fivethirtyeight .com/features/dont-hold-your-breath-for-gender-parity-in-congress-it-could-take -another-100-years/.

"Sister Rosetta Tharpe." Rock & Roll Hall of Fame. 2018. https://www.rockhall.com /nominee/sister-rosetta-tharpe.

Sive, Rebecca. *Every Day Is Election Day: A Woman's Guide to Winning Any Office, from the PTA to the White House*. Chicago: Chicago Review Press, 2013.

Smith, Allan. "Melania Trump Responds: 'Unacceptable and Offensive to Me.'" *Business Insider*, October 8, 2016. http://www.businessinsider.com/melania-trump-donald -leaked-tape-2016-10.

Smith, Margaret Chase. "Declaration of Conscience." US Senate, June 1, 1950. https://www.senate.gov/artandhistory/history/resources/pdf/SmithDeclaration.pdf

"Smith, Margaret Chase." US House of Representatives History, Art & Archives. Accessed February 5, 2018. http://history.house.gov/People/Detail/21866.

Solis, Marie. "A Record Number of Women Are Running for Governor in 2018." *Newsweek*, January 2, 2018. http://www.newsweek.com/record-number-women -are-running-governor-2018-768018.

Solis, Marie. "Tammy Duckworth May Have to Breastfeed in a Bathroom Off the Senate Floor, Says Former Senate Parliamentarian." *Newsweek*, February 15, 2018. http://www.newsweek.com/tammy-duckworth-may-have-breastfeed-bathroom -senate-floor-says-former-senate-807393.

"Southern Christian Leadership Conference (SCLC)." The Martin Luther King, Jr. Research and Education Institute at Stanford University, January 10, 1957. http://kingencyclopedia.stanford.edu/encyclopedia/enc_southern _christian_leadership_conference_sclc/.

Sprague, Leah W. "Her Life: The Woman Behind the New Deal." Frances Perkins Center, June 1, 2014. http://francesperkinscenter.org/life-new/.

State Elections Offices. "Official 2016 Presidential General Election Results." January 30, 2017. https://transition.fec.gov/pubrec/fe2016/2016presgeresults.pdf.

"Statue History: Engineering, Construction, and Crossing the Atlantic." The Statue of Liberty – Ellis Island Foundation. https://www.libertyellisfoundation.org /statue-history.

Stolberg, Sheryl Gay. "'It's About Time': A Baby Comes to the Senate Floor." *New York Times*, April 19, 2018. https://www.nytimes.com/2018/04/19/us/politics/baby -duckworth-senate-floor.html.

Stolberg, Sheryl Gay. "Proof That Women Are the Better Dealmakers in the Senate." *New York Times*, February 19, 2015. https://www.nytimes.com/politics/first-draft /2015/02/19/in-the-senate-women-are-better-dealmakers-than-men-heres-proof/.

Sturkey, William. "The 1964 Mississippi Freedom Schools." *Mississippi History Now*, May 2016. http://www.mshistorynow.mdah.ms.gov/articles/403/The-1964 -Mississippi-Freedom-Schools.

Tackett, Michael. "White Evangelical Women, Core Supporters of Trump, Begin Tiptoeing Away." *New York Times*, March 11, 2018. https://www.nytimes.com /2018/03/11/us/politics/white-evangelical-women-trump.html.

Taylor v. Louisiana, 419 U.S. 522 (1975).

Terkel, Studs. *Division Street: America.* New York: Pantheon Books, 1967.

Thanawala, Sudhin. "$25M Deal Over Trump University Fraud Lawsuits Moves Forward." Associated Press, February 6, 2018. https://apnews.com/43033e7cb9974faf879b 51251c3a0d07.

The Association of the Bar of the City of New York. *Year Book 1974.* New York, 1974.

"Thomas Paine Biography." Biography.com. Accessed June 6, 2018. https://www .biography.com/people/thomas-paine-9431951.

Thompson, Krissah. "Houston's Annise Parker, A Gay Mayor in a Red State, Ponders Political Future." *Washington Post*, March 17, 2015. https://www.washingtonpost .com/lifestyle/style/houstons-annise-parker-a-gay-mayor-in-a-red-state-ponders -political-future/2015/03/17/c06c8b3e-c7f1-11e4-a199-6cb5e63819d2_story.html.

Tully, Shawn. "Donald Trump Got a Tax Break For Stiffing Contractors." *Fortune*, October 8, 2016. http://fortune.com/2016/10/08/donald-trump-taxes-contractors/.

"Transcript: Donald Trump's Taped Comments about Women." *New York Times*, October 8, 2016. https://www.nytimes.com/2016/10/08/us/donald-trump-tape -transcript.html.

Trickey, Erick. "The Story Behind a Forgotten Symbol of the American Revolution: The Liberty Tree." Smithsonian.com, May 19, 2016. https://www.smithsonianmag.com /history/story-behind-forgotten-symbol-american-revolution-liberty-tree-180959162/.

Tumulty, Karen. "'If We Don't Run, Then We Won't Achieve.' Why a Record Number of Women Are Eyeing a Run for Governor." *Washington Post*, January 1, 2018. https://www.washingtonpost.com/politics/if-we-dont-run-then-we-wont-achieve -why-a-record-number-of-women-are-eyeing-a-run-for-governor/2018/01/01 /10938cf4-e674-11e7-a65d-1ac0fd7f097e_story.html.

US Census Bureau. "The Majority of Children Live With Two Parents, Census Bureau Reports." Press release, November 17, 2016. https://www.census.gov/newsroom /press-releases/2016/cb16-192.html.

Valencia, Anna (Chicago city clerk). Interview by the author, February 2018.

"Vi's Experience & Key Accomplishments." Vi Lyles for Mayor website. Accessed June 6, 2018. https://vilyles.com/experience-accomplishments/.

Volden, Craig, Alan E. Wiseman, and Dana E. Wittmer. "Women's Issues and Their Fates in the US Congress." *Political Science Research and Methods* (July 8, 2016): 1–18. https://doi.org/10.1017/psrm.2016.32.

Walker, Marcia. "Wyatt, Rev. Addie (1924–2012)." BlackPast.org. http://www.blackpast .org/aah/wyatt-rev-addie-1924-2012.

Wang, Amy B. "'Nevertheless, She Persisted' Becomes New Battle Cry After McConnell Silences Elizabeth Warren." *Washington Post*, February 8, 2017. https://www .washingtonpost.com/news/the-fix/wp/2017/02/08/nevertheless-she-persisted -becomes-new-battle-cry-after-mcconnell-silen.

Wang, Jennifer. "The Richest Women in the World 2018." *Forbes*, March 6, 2018. https:// www.forbes.com/sites/jenniferwang/2018/03/06/richest-women/#787a6d6e81f1.

Warner, Judith, and Danielle Corley. "The Women's Leadership Gap." Center for American Progress, May 21, 2017. https://www.americanprogress.org/issues /women/reports/2017/05/21/432758/womens-leadership-gap/.

Wells, Ida B. "Lynch Law in All Its Phases." Voices of Democracy: The US Oratory Project, transcribed from speech on February 13, 1893. http://voicesofdemocracy .umd.edu/wells-lynch-law-speech-text.

Wells, Ida B., and Alfreda M. Duster, ed. *Crusade for Justice: The Autobiography of Ida B. Wells*. Chicago: University of Chicago Press, 1970.

Wheeler, Lydia. "Ginsburg Appears to Wear 'Dissent' Collar on Bench." *Hill*, November 9, 2016. thehill.com/blogs/blog-briefing-room/news/305246-ginsburg-appears-to -wear-dissent-collar-on-bench.

"Whirlpool Corporation: Global Locations," Whirlpool Corporation website. http://www.whirlpoolcorp.com/global-locations/.

White House Office of the First Lady. "Transcript: Michelle Obama's Speech on Donald Trump's Alleged Treatment of Women." NPR, October 13, 2016. https://www .npr.org/2016/10/13/497846667/transcript-michelle-obamas-speech-on-donald -trumps-alleged-treatment-of-women.

Williams, Joe. "All 22 Female Senators Demand Leadership Acts on Sexual Harassment Legislation." *Roll Call*, March 28, 2018. https://www.rollcall.com/news/politics/all -22-women-senators-press-leadership-to-move-on-sexual-harassment-legislation.

Williams, Vanessa. "Report: Black Women Underrepresented in Elected Offices, But Could Make Gains and History in 2018." *Washington Post*, March 5, 2018. https://www.washingtonpost.com/news/post-nation/wp/2018/03/05/black-women-looking-to-make-history-increase-their-numbers-in-elected-offices-in-2018/.

Willis, Ellen. *No More Nice Girls: Countercultural Essays*. Hanover, NH: University Press of New England for Wesleyan University Press, 1992.

Wolfers, Justin. "Fewer Women Run Big Companies Than Men Named John." *New York Times*, March 2, 2015. https://www.nytimes.com/2015/03/03/upshot/fewer-women-run-big-companies-than-men-named-john.html.

"Women in Elective Office 2018." Center for American Women and Politics. http://www.cawp.rutgers.edu/women-elective-office-2018.

"Women in Statewide Elective Executive Office 2018." Center for American Women and Politics. http://www.cawp.rutgers.edu/women-statewide-elective-executive-office-2018.

"Women Mayors in US Cities 2018." Center for American Women and Politics. http://www.cawp.rutgers.edu/levels_of_office/women-mayors-us-cities-2018.

World Economic Forum. *The Global Gender Gap Report 2017*. November 2, 2017. https://www.weforum.org/reports/the-global-gender-gap-report-2017.

Yglesias, Matthew. "What Really Happened in 2016, in 7 Charts." *Vox*, September 18, 2017. https://www.vox.com/policy-and-politics/2017/9/18/16305486/what-really-happened-in-2016.

Zakaria, Fareed. "Hillary Clinton: Misogyny Is Endemic." *CNN*, October 15, 2017. https://www.cnn.com/videos/tv/2017/10/15/exp-clinton-misogyny.cnn.

Zaklikowski, Dovid. "Turning Disappointment into Food for the Hungry." TheRebbe.org. Accessed April 1, 2018. https://www.chabad.org/therebbe/article_cdo/aid/558041/jewish/Turning-Disappointment-into-Food-for-the-Hungry.htm.

ACKNOWLEDGMENTS

I thank my parents, Mary and David Sive, for their encouragement of my interest in politics and public service. I wish my father could have lived long enough to help me with this book, as he did with my first, but he still inspired me as I wrote.

Julia Stasch and I have been friends since graduate school and have worked on many women's projects together. I am very grateful to Julia for writing the foreword to *Vote Her In* and sharing her wisdom with us.

Kim Foxx, Lisa Madigan, and Anna Valencia are among a group of amazing and generous women in politics who have blazed a trail for every woman. I am grateful for the opportunity to collaborate with them and thank them for the sage advice they share here. They were ably assisted by Robert Foley for State's Attorney Foxx; Kate Le Furgy for Clerk Valencia; and Maura Possley for Attorney General Madigan.

Great friends and colleagues helped make this book possible, including the people at Agate Publishing: Doug Seibold, Jessica Easto, Morgan Krehbiel, Jacqueline Jarik, and Deirdre Kennedy; Mike Lenehan, a wise counselor; Samantha Loo and Toni Shears, who assisted me with manuscript preparation; Trevor Albert, Diane Alexander, Pam Cummings, Fatima Goss Graves, Jen Hoyt, Gayden Metcalfe, Erica Mann Ramis, Julia Reed, Alison Riley, Laurie Rubiner, and Leila Wynn, who offered their generous personal support; and all those who graciously endorsed *Vote Her In*, including Katherine Baicker, Heather Booth, Kim Foxx, Linda Hirshman, Lisa Madigan, Ruth Mandel, Robin Marty, Anne Moses, Helaine Olen, Toni Preckwinkle, Aviva Rosman, Julie Scelfo, Jan Schakowsky, Jessica Spring and Chandler O'Leary, Anna Valencia, Erin Vilardi, and Jessica Yellin.

No guide to women's activism is possible without the devotion and work of women everywhere, who make the time to change the world. In this case, I extend my deepest thanks to the world's women marchers and the great artists among them, who have inspired the rest of us everywhere and inspire me every day.

ABOUT THE AUTHOR

Rebecca Sive has held executive positions in business, government, philanthropy, and nonprofit management. She received a gubernatorial appointment to become a founding member of the Illinois Human Rights Commission, and she has been recognized by her alma maters, Carleton College and the University of Illinois, for her distinguished community leadership. Sive was a founding board member of the Chicago Foundation for Women and was part of a national group of women leaders who developed women's issues agendas for Presidents Bill Clinton and Barack Obama. She is the author of *Every Day Is Election Day: A Woman's Guide to Winning Any Office, from the PTA to the White House,* and she has taught at the University of Chicago Harris School of Public Policy. Sive lives in Chicago, Illinois, and Keeler Township, Michigan.